TRUSTING
the covenant

Participant Guide

Episodes 17–24

COVENANT BIBLE STUDY
TRUSTING THE COVENANT: PARTICIPANT GUIDE

Copyright © 2014 by Abingdon Press

All rights reserved.

No part of this work may be reproduced or transmitted in any form or by any means, electronic or mechanical, including photocopying and recording, or by any information storage or retrieval system, except as may be expressly permitted by the 1976 Copyright Act or in writing from the publisher. Requests for permission should be addressed to Permissions, Abingdon Press, 2222 Rosa L. Parks Blvd., PO Box 280988, Nashville, TN 37228-0988 or permissions@abingdonpress.org.

This book is printed on acid-free paper.

ISBN 978-1-4267-7218-4

Scripture quotations are from the Common English Bible. Copyright © 2011 by the Common English Bible. All rights reserved. Used by permission. www.CommonEnglishBible.com.

Printed in the United States of America

17 18 19 20 21 22 23—10 9 8 7 6 5 4 3 2

Covenant Bible Study resources include:

Creating, Living, and Trusting Participant Guides, ISBN 978-1-5018-4015-9
Creating the Covenant: Participant Guide, ISBN 978-1-4267-7216-0 (large print ISBN 978-1-63088-625-7)
Living the Covenant: Participant Guide, ISBN 978-1-4267-7217-7 (large print ISBN 978-1-63088-626-4)
Trusting the Covenant: Participant Guide, ISBN 978-1-4267-7218-4 (large print ISBN 978-1-63088-627-1)

Covenant Bible Study: Covenant Meditations, ISBN 978-1-4267-7220-7
Covenant Bible Study: Covenant Meditations ePub, ISBN 978-1-4267-7221-4

Covenant Bible Study: Leader Guide, ISBN 978-1-4267-7223-8
Covenant Bible Study: Leader Guide ePub, ISBN 978-1-4267-7225-2

Covenant Bible Study: DVD Video (set of three), ISBN 978-1-4267-8678-5
Covenant Bible Study: MP4 Video Episodes (download individually from CovenantBibleStudy.com)

CEB Study Bible, hardcover ISBN 978-1-6092-6028-6, decotone ISBN 978-1-6092-6040-8
CEB Study Bible: Large Print Edition, hardcover ISBN 978-1-60926-176-4

To order resources or to obtain additional information for participants, Covenant groups, and leaders, go to www.CovenantBibleStudy.com or to www.cokesbury.com. All print resources are available exclusively from these online sites, from Cokesbury reps, or by calling Cokesbury (800-672-1789).

TRUSTING
the covenant

Contents

Trusting the Covenant

Episode	Theme	Title	Page
17	Life Together	John; 1, 2, and 3 John	9
18	Praise and Lament	Psalms	21
19	Tragedy	Job	31
20	Crisis and Starting Over	Jeremiah, Lamentations, Ezekiel	41
21	Exile and Renewal	Isaiah 40–66	53
22	Restoration	1 and 2 Chronicles, Ezra, Nehemiah	65
23	Hope	Apocalyptic: Daniel	75
24	New Creation	Revelation	85

Other Covenant Participant Guides

Creating the Covenant

Episode	Theme	Title	Page
1	Relationships	Creating the Covenant	11
2	Who Are We?	Torah: Genesis	21
3	Freedom and Instruction	Exodus, Leviticus, Numbers	31
4	God's Kingdom	Gospels: Matthew and Mark	41
5	Grace	Letters: Romans and Galatians	51
6	Witness	Hebrews	63
7	Logic of the Cross	1 and 2 Corinthians	71
8	Covenant Renewal	Deuteronomy, Joshua, Judges, 1 Samuel	83

Living the Covenant

Episode	Theme	Title	Page
9	Faithful Love	Ruth, Esther, Song of Songs	9
10	The Spirit-Led Community	Luke and Acts	21
11	Leadership	2 Samuel, 1 and 2 Kings	33
12	God's Household	1 and 2 Thessalonians, 1 and 2 Timothy, Titus	43
13	Discernment	Wisdom: Proverbs and Ecclesiastes	55
14	Reconciled	Philemon, Philippians, Colossians, Ephesians	65
15	Act Like a Christian	James, Jude, 1 and 2 Peter	75
16	Doing the Right Thing	Prophets: Isaiah 1–39 and the Book of the Twelve	85

the covenant

Covenant Group Participants and Leader

Name　　　　　　　　　　　**Phone**　　　　　　　　　　　**E-mail**

_____

_____

_____

_____

_____

_____

_____

_____

_____

_____

_____

_____

_____

Covenant Group Meeting Location _____

Covenant Group Meeting Day and Time _____

CovenantBibleStudy.com username _____ password _____

Bible Readings at a Glance

Sign up with your group at CovenantBibleStudy.com to get daily readings by e-mail from your group leader.

Episode 17

Day 1	John 1:1-18; 3–4	God's children love the light.	❏
Day 2	John 5; 9; 11	From healing to discipleship	❏
Day 3	John 14–17	So that they will be made perfectly one	❏
Day 4	John 18–21	Resurrection community	❏
Day 5	1 John 2–4; 2 John; 3 John	Hospitality is Christian love in action.	❏
Day 6	Covenant Meditation on John 15:9-13	Living well for others	❏
Day 7	Group Meeting Experience with John 13:1-17	Foot washing	❏

Episode 18

Day 1	Psalms 1–2; 19; 119:1-42	God's expectations	❏
Day 2	Psalms 13; 22; 80; 90	Desperate prayer for help	❏
Day 3	Psalms 34; 107; 116; 138	Giving thanks	❏
Day 4	Psalms 8; 104; 148	Creation songs	❏
Day 5	Psalms 146–150	Hallelujah!	❏
Day 6	Covenant Meditation on Psalm 139:1-6	Lord, you know me.	❏
Day 7	Group Meeting Experience with Psalm 42	Like a deer that craves streams of water	❏

Episode 19

☐	Day 1	Job 1–2	Job's story
☐	Day 2	Job 3; 9; 19; 31	Job's response
☐	Day 3	Job 4–5; 8; 11	The friends' arguments
☐	Day 4	Job 38–41	God's speeches from the whirlwind
☐	Day 5	Job 42; reread Job 1–2	Job's response to God and the epilogue
☐	Day 6	Covenant Meditation on Job 2	What do you say to a friend in pain?
☐	Day 7	Group Meeting Experience with Job 42:7-17	Double for his trouble?

Episode 20

☐	Day 1	Jeremiah 1–4	Jeremiah's call and Judah's disregard of the covenant
☐	Day 2	Jeremiah 27–29	Living under Babylonian rule
☐	Day 3	Jeremiah 16; 18–20	Jeremiah's lament for himself and for his people
☐	Day 4	Lamentations 1–2; 5	The people's call for help
☐	Day 5	Ezekiel 34–37	Ezekiel's visions of transformation; a new covenant
☐	Day 6	Covenant Meditation on Lamentations 3:1-24	Living with crisis
☐	Day 7	Group Meeting Experience with Jeremiah 31:15-34	The new covenant

Episode 21

☐	Day 1	Isaiah 40–43	Creation
☐	Day 2	Isaiah 49:1–52:12	Comfort
☐	Day 3	Isaiah 52:13–55:13	Restoration
☐	Day 4	Isaiah 56:1-8; 58–61	Justice
☐	Day 5	Isaiah 63:7–66:24	Presence
☐	Day 6	Covenant Meditation on Isaiah 43:1-7	Hope comes from God.
☐	Day 7	Group Meeting Experience with Isaiah 40:12-31	God as creator of the world and of Israel

Episode 22

Day 1	1 Chronicles 10:1–11:9; 28–29	The temple at the center of the community	❏
Day 2	2 Chronicles 33–36	Return and restoration	❏
Day 3	Ezra 1; 2:68–6:22	Rebuilding	❏
Day 4	Ezra 7–10	Ezra continues the restoration.	❏
Day 5	Nehemiah 1–2; 4; 7:73b–8:18	Nehemiah rebuilds walls; Ezra renews the covenant.	❏
Day 6	Covenant Meditation on 2 Chronicles 15:12-15	Don't abandon each other!	❏
Day 7	Group Meeting Experience with 1 Chronicles 29:10-19	David's prayer	❏

Episode 23

Day 1	Daniel 1–2	The emperor's dream	❏
Day 2	Daniel 3–4	The emperor's madness	❏
Day 3	Daniel 6	Civil disobedience	❏
Day 4	Daniel 7	Fifth monarchy	❏
Day 5	Daniel 9	Daniel's prayer	❏
Day 6	Covenant Meditation on Daniel 9:4-19	Trusting the covenant	❏
Day 7	Group Meeting Experience with Daniel 11:27-35	What about apocalyptic visions?	❏

Episode 24

Day 1	Revelation 1–3	John is called.	❏
Day 2	Revelation 4:1–8:1	Opening the scroll	❏
Day 3	Revelation 12–14	Defeating evil	❏
Day 4	Revelation 15–17	Seven plagues	❏
Day 5	Revelation 19–22	Final destination	❏
Day 6	Covenant Meditation on Revelation 7:9-17	Making us new	❏
Day 7	Group Meeting Experience	Our covenant	❏

the covenant

Covenant Creative Team

Editorial
Theodore Hiebert, Old Testament Editor
Jaime Clark-Soles, New Testament Editor
Magrey deVega, Leadership Editor
Pam Hawkins, Meditations Editor
David Teel, Project Manager
Paul Franklyn, General Editor and Associate Publisher
Neil M. Alexander, Publisher

Video Cohosts
Christine Chakoian, Senior Pastor,
   First Presbyterian Church, Lake Forest, IL
Shane Stanford, Senior Pastor,
   Christ United Methodist Church, Memphis, TN

Writers: Trusting the Covenant

Episode 17   Jaime Clark-Soles, Associate Professor of New Testament, Perkins School of Theology, Dallas, TX

Episode 18   William P. Brown, William Marcellus McPheeters Professor of Old Testament, Columbia Theological Seminary, Decatur, GA

Episode 19   Amy Erickson, Assistant Professor of Hebrew Bible, Iliff School of Theology, Denver, CO

Episode 20   Linda M. Day, Assistant Professor of Old Testament and Chaplain, Hiram College, Hiram, OH

Episode 21   Patricia K. Tull, A. B. Rhodes Professor of Old Testament, Louisville Presbyterian Theological Seminary, Louisville, KY

Episode 22   Melody D. Knowles, Vice President of Academic Affairs and Associate Professor of Old Testament, Virginia Theological Seminary, Alexandria, VA

Episode 23   Daniel L. Smith-Christopher, Professor of Theological Studies, Loyola Marymount College, Los Angeles, CA

Episode 24   Thomas B. Slater, Professor of New Testament Language and Literature, McAfee School of Theology, Atlanta, GA

Production and Design
Christy Lynch, Production Editor
Jeff Moore, Packaging and Interior Design
Emily Keafer Lambright, Interior Design
PerfecType, Typesetting

CovenantBibleStudy.com
Christie Durand, Analyst
Gregory Davis, Developer
David Burns, Designer
Dan Heile, Database Analyst

Video Production: Revolution Pictures, Inc.
Randy Brewer, Executive Producer
Michelle Abnet, Producer
Ry Cox, Codirector
Jeff Venable, Codirector
Chris Adams, Photography Director
Brandon Eller, Prop Master
Dave Donnelly, Post Editor
Perry Trest, Colorist

EPISODE 17

John; 1, 2, and 3 John

LIFE TOGETHER
Abundant, eternal life with others

Bible Readings

Day 1: John 1:1-18; 3–4
Day 2: John 5; 9; 11
Day 3: John 14–17
Day 4: John 18–21
Day 5: 1 John 2–4; 2 John; 3 John
Day 6: Covenant Meditation on John 15:9-13
Day 7: Group Meeting Experience with John 13:1-17

Covenant Prayer

For those who walk in darkness

The word was life, and the life was the light for all people. (John 1:4)

For those who flourish for others

This is the testimony: God gave eternal life to us, and this life is in his Son. (1 John 5:11)

OUR LONGING FOR RELATIONSHIP

We are created to be in relationship—with God and with God's creation. Our tendency to separate from God and others disrupts the rhythms of life and leaves us unsettled, undone, and unsure.

JOHN'S GOSPEL

John's Gospel points us to an authentic community characterized by trust, intimacy, love, and abundant, eternal life. The purpose of the Gospel is clearly stated in John 20:31: "These things are written so that you will believe that Jesus is the Christ, God's Son, and that believing, you will have life in his name." The fourth Gospel is a narrative, not a newspaper account. John writes not simply to convey information but to draw you into an encounter with the risen Christ, into a relationship that from then onward will shape every minute of your precious life—every thought, deed, habit, and desire.

John's Gospel was written in stages over decades, taking its final form in approximately 100 CE. This makes it the last Gospel of the four in our New Testament, and right away you'll notice that it's quite different from the other three Gospels (Matthew, Mark, and Luke), called Synoptic Gospels because they share many phrases and stories in common. (A good tool for comparing the phrases and stories in these books is the *CEB Gospel Parallels*.) We avoid trying to force John into the framework of the Synoptic Gospels. More than 90 percent of John's content doesn't appear in the Synoptics. Many of the dearly loved stories about individuals who encounter Jesus (Nicodemus, the Samaritan woman, Lazarus, Thomas) appear only in John. Sometimes we see characters who appear elsewhere, but the particular stories about them told in John are stunningly unique (Mary and Martha, Mary Magdalene, Peter, Thomas). Events sometimes even occur in a different order: In John, the "temple tantrum" occurs at the beginning, not the end, of Jesus' public ministry. Jesus also dies on a different day in John. Don't fret over the differences, but instead ask what John is trying to signify through his way of presenting the story.

John is obsessed with the power of words, so much so that he identifies Jesus as the Word (Greek *logos*). Words can surely lead to life. In John 6, Jesus speaks difficult words that cause him to lose many disciples. At that point he turns to his other disciples and asks them if they, too, would like to leave their committed community. Peter responds, "Lord, where would we go? You have the words of eternal life" (John 6:68).

But words can destroy, as well. That's why any responsible study of the fourth Gospel requires a word of warning about the role of "the Jews" in the narrative. Obviously, Jesus and all of the first disciples were Jewish, as was the early Johannine community. Before the destruction of the temple in 70 CE, Christianity was another form

---

John is obsessed with the power of words, so much so that he identifies Jesus as the Word (Greek logos*). Words can surely lead to life.*

of Judaism. But after the destruction of the temple, Christianity began the lengthy process of becoming a separate tradition. As that happened, sadly, this separation sometimes led to Christians using John's Gospel to insult or harm Jews because the original historical context of the Gospel's composition wasn't properly and intelligently tended. To avoid anti-Semitism, unintended or otherwise, the CEB translates the phrase *the Jews* as "Jewish leaders" or "religious leaders" to indicate that the debate was between the Jewish establishment and the Jewish reformers (for example, Jesus of Nazareth).

When the Gospel reached its final draft, the community that read John's story consisted of an amazingly diverse population in terms of culture, religion, race, and ethnicity: Jews, Samaritans, Gentiles, John the Baptist's former followers, Greeks, and Romans. Such diversity is always a gift and sometimes a challenge.

The fourth Gospel engages us with a masterful literary design:

Prologue—John 1:1-18: This rich text reveals much about who Jesus is and who we are in relation to God and each other. Think about how Genesis begins (covered in Episode 2). The prologue establishes all of the major themes that matter to John; everything after 1:18 fills in the details.

The Book of Signs—John 1:19–12:50: This section tells about Jesus' public ministry. He performs seven signs in John (as compared to approximately twenty signs in Mark), and they are never called miracles or deeds of power. They are signs, and signs point to something. In John, they point to the fact that Jesus is equal to God and, therefore, has power to grant life even in the face of death, especially in the face of death.

The Book of Glory—John 13:1–20:31: At this point in the narrative, Jesus turns inward to train his closest disciples as he prepares for his crucifixion, exaltation, and glorification on the cross. The words *glory* and *glorify* appear forty-two times in John, far more than in any other book of the New Testament, and they congregate in these later chapters. Jesus is not a victim—he knows what he has come to do and does it all with calm and peace.

Epilogue—John 21:1-25: John's Gospel has two endings. The first occurs at John 20:31. Chapter 21 was probably added later, perhaps by the same author or perhaps by a later editor. The last chapter is deeply poignant and speaks to our various diverse callings, including our tendency to get into competition with each other even as disciples; the importance of love in action; and the potential sacrifice and humility involved in answering Christ's call.

As you move forward in accordance with God's will, do you proceed deliberately with calm and peace? Jot down some thoughts about when you proceeded with confidence in helping others or standing up for the right thing.

1, 2, and 3 John: The letters of John reflect a later phase of the community that produced and read John's Gospel. We don't know whether all three letters were written by the same person (the elder) or whether that person had a hand in writing the fourth Gospel. Thematically speaking, the letters care about many of the same issues that we saw in the Gospel: testifying to truth, believing in Jesus as the incarnate Word, and unity among believers. Upon what should that unity be based? Doctrine, behavior, or love? How are those three related?

> **Optional:** *An additional video on incarnation and abundant love is available for download from* **CovenantBibleStudy.com**.

But most importantly, the letters announce God's love for us (1 John 4:19), the call to love each other (1 John 4:11), and the promise that fear is not our fate: "There is no fear in love, but perfect love drives out fear, because fear expects punishment. The person who is afraid has not been made perfect in love" (1 John 4:18).

Day 1: John 1:1-18; 3–4
God's children love the light.

When you read John 1:1-18 in the CEB, you will see that it's indented and presented in poetic form because it's a hymn. If you compare John's opening to those of the Synoptic Gospels (Matthew, Mark, and Luke), you will see that John goes back farther than anyone else, to the very beginning when God and Jesus created every single thing that exists. Jesus is presented in terms of Woman Wisdom, whom John would have known from Proverbs 8. She tries to teach wisdom through the Instruction (Torah), but people tend to prefer foolishness, even though that path never leads to life. But those who do listen to Wisdom, to God's Word, become enlightened by the light of the world and enjoy life as children in God's household.

> **Optional:** *Additional videos retelling the stories of Nicodemus, and Jesus and the Samaritan woman at the well, are available for download from* **CovenantBibleStudy.com**.

Not long after the prologue we meet Nicodemus, who comes to Jesus "by night" and hears about being born from above. He misunderstands and is stuck at the literal level, wondering how he might be born again, a second time. But Jesus is speaking metaphorically. He appears again in John 7:50 and John 19:39-42 (where he is once again identified as the one who came by night).

Does Nicodemus ever see the light? If not, what stands in his way? If so, how does it affect his life?

The next individual to encounter Jesus is the Samaritan woman in John 4. Unlike Nicodemus, she encounters Jesus in the brightest light of day, at noon. Notice that she engages Jesus in a theological debate and, as a result, receives a revelation that Jesus is God (John 4:26). She then immediately testifies to her neighbors and invites them to encounter Jesus for themselves.

Why is the time of these meetings, night or day, a crucial detail, given what has been said in John 3:17-21?

Day 2: John 5; 9; 11
From healing to discipleship

These chapters share the idea that Jesus provides healing, but the stories differ in certain ways. Compare the behavior of the man in John 5 to the behavior of the Samaritan woman one chapter earlier (John's placement of material isn't accidental) and the behavior of the blind man in John 9. Both the Samaritan woman and the blind man are models for the kind of discipleship that John has in mind. John 9 opens with the disciples revealing their assumption that illness is caused by sin. Throughout the chapter, Jesus reorients our vision to show us what true sin and true blindness are: the willful rejection of God and of abundant life, and resignation to existence in a dark, dank spiritual tomb where fear, death, and violence reign.

What makes the blind man an exemplary disciple? First, he is open to the creative power of Jesus: When Jesus spits and makes mud and wipes it on the man's eyes, we are supposed to remember the Genesis story where God uses the earth to create human beings. Second, the man tells his truth as he knows it, and he never allows anyone—the neighbors, the educated or powerful religious authorities, not even his own family members—to deny his own experience. He keeps his integrity throughout, no matter what the cost. Third, he publicly testifies to his healing relationship with Jesus. Fourth, the more he encounters Jesus, the deeper his knowledge and faith become. He first calls Jesus just a man (John 9:11), then a prophet (John 9:17), and finally he proclaims, "Lord, I believe," and worships him (John 9:38).

Compare this story about the blind man with John 11.

Day 3: John 14–17
So that they will be made perfectly one

John 14–17 is known as the farewell speech. Here Jesus teaches the disciples everything they will need to know to be mature Christian leaders who can create spaces for healthy, authentic, and fruitful communities of dearly loved disciples. In John 14 he assures them that though he will no longer physically be with them, he is always present, as is the Companion. Against the notion that God, Jesus, and the Holy Spirit are "up there" somewhere, and that we will all eventually get a room in God's heavenly resort, Jesus once again insists that the movement is always in the other direction. God has always come to us and is always coming to us. In John's Gospel, Jesus is described as "the one who is coming into the world" (John 11:27). There is no separation between heaven and earth (see John 1:51). As Jesus says of himself and God in John 14:23, "we will come to them and make our home with them."

In John 15, Jesus warns the disciples that their future won't be easy, but as long as they love each other and stay connected to him, they will experience peace and joy, even in the midst of the world's hatred. The discourse concludes with Jesus' prayer on behalf of his disciples, then and now, that we may all be one in Christ expressly for the sake of the world (John 17:20-21)—the very world that may hate them.

Think of a difficult time in your life. Did you experience peace and joy by loving someone else and staying connected in thought and prayer to Jesus?

Day 4: John 18–21
Resurrection community

In John 14:6, Jesus confidently declares himself to be the way, the truth, and the life. Yet by John 19:30, the truth is put on trial and killed at the hands of the same Pilate who had recently wondered aloud to Jesus, "What is truth?" After birthing the church at the foot of the cross (John 19:25-27), blood and water come out of Jesus' side—and one is reminded of all the language in John about birth and wombs (John 3:4; 7:38; 16:21). Then one thinks of our rituals for baptism and holy communion. All the makings of being in God's family are there, but Jesus' followers are too blinded by grief and fear to move forward into their future story. Only Mary Magdalene ventures to the tomb and finds it empty. Peter and the dearly loved disciple come to see for themselves, but they go back home. Mary remains, stays put, and, by doing so, she receives the first vision of the resurrected Christ and becomes the apostle to the apostles, proclaiming the good news to her community. The disciples fearfully lock themselves in a room, but nothing can separate us from Christ, so Jesus appears to grant them peace and the gift of the Holy Spirit that he had promised earlier. So what do the disciples do? They go back to living their pre-Jesus life. Again, Jesus comes to them. He frees Peter from his shame and infuses them with a sense of calling. They answered it, and the world hasn't been the same since.

If we acknowledge that each person can find a calling or purpose in life, what calling gives you purpose? What type of service or ministry is engaged through that calling?

> **Optional:** *An additional video retelling the story of Mary Magdalene at the tomb is available for download from* **CovenantBibleStudy.com**.

Day 5: 1 John 2–4; 2 John; 3 John
Hospitality is Christian love in action.

The Johannine letters worry about Christians who deny the incarnation, the fleshly nature of Jesus, preferring to keep him an abstract doctrine. The author knows that the minute we deny the true humanity of Jesus and the scandal of that uncomfortable, messy truth, we are also likely to turn our eyes away from the true humanity of each other. Incarnation means that Jesus had flesh and blood like us and that we, too, live on this earth embodied and located in very specific circumstances, including our gender, sexuality, race, class, ethnicity, and levels of able-bodiedness.

Do we value certain bodies more than others in our society? In our church?

Surely these letters teach us about Christian hospitality, which is love in action. We see this in 1 John 3:17: "If a person has material possessions and sees a brother or sister in need and that person doesn't care—how can the love of God remain in him?" Compare 3 John 1:5: "Dear friend, you act faithfully in whatever you do for our brothers and sisters, even though they are strangers." Since there was no hotel system in the New Testament era and certainly no welfare system, Christians depended on each other for sustenance, and Christian travelers stayed with other Christians as they traveled.

But the letters display a real tension between hospitality and hatred, between orthodoxy and tolerance. For every verse that commands hospitality, one finds a verse that commands one to refuse hospitality to those who don't subscribe to proper belief (see 2 John 1:10-11). The letters reveal the tendency for disagreements to lead to schism. It is clear from 1 John 2:18-19 that this church has experienced the painful loss of some of its members. The author goes on the attack and declares those who left to be antichrists and deceivers.

Is it inevitable that Christians (or even human beings) consistently choose sides over issues so that the choice is either/or? Reflect on a situation where someone left a church or a group where you participated. What might have prevented that separation?

Instead we can rely upon the truth expressed, ironically, by the very same author just a few verses earlier: "The person loving a brother and sister stays in the light, and there is nothing in the light that causes a person to stumble. But the person who hates a brother or sister is in the darkness and lives in the darkness, and doesn't know where to go because the darkness blinds the eyes" (1 John 2:10-11).

Day 6: John 15:9-13
Covenant Meditation: Living well for others

Today's practice focuses on reading scripture in a structured, prayerful way in order to grow more attuned to God's presence in our daily lives. The classic name for this ancient pattern of praying the scriptures is *lectio divina*, which in Latin means "divine reading." Traditionally in *lectio divina*, there are four key movements through which we listen to a brief selection of scripture: reading, meditating, praying, and resting (contemplating) in God's word.

Our passage for today is John 15:9-13, in which Jesus addresses the essence of living well for others by experiencing God's love. Open your Bible to this scripture and mark its location. Get comfortable where you are seated, placing both feet on the ground and letting your breathing calm.

Read the passage slowly, aloud or silently, paying attention to the whole text—every sentence, phrase, and word. Approach the scripture as though it is new to you. When finished, wait in a minute of silence.

Read the passage again, now listening for one word or phrase that catches your attention. Try not to analyze why a specific word or phrase stands out to you, but receive it as something God invites you to hear. If desired, write this word or phrase in your participant guide. Take three minutes of silence to reflect on what has caught your attention. What does this word or phrase bring to mind for you? Let your mind engage with the word or phrase, and consider what it means to you right now. Resist editing your thoughts.

Read the scripture one last time. Now reflect on feelings or memories your word or phrase evokes. Does your word or phrase point to something that you or someone you know longs for or needs? In as much or as little silent time as you need, write down any reflections that come to your mind or heart.

When you are ready, offer back in prayer to God all that you have heard, thought, and felt in this spiritual reading practice. Entrust to God any insights, questions, worries, and longings that this scripture brings to light for you. Before you end this time of praying the scripture, ask yourself if you sense an invitation from God to act or respond in some way. There may be a small invitation (to check on a friend) or a broad one (to begin to recycle), or you may not yet sense an invitation. Stay open to the possibility that in the days ahead, an invitation may be revealed through this reading. Offer God thanks, and end the practice with "Amen."

Group Meeting Experience

John 13:1-17 | *Foot washing*

We noted in the introduction that John 1–12 can be called the book of signs. That's where Jesus performs his public ministry. Chapter 12 ends with the story about Mary, the sister of Martha and Lazarus (not Mary Magdalene and not the sinful woman from the other Gospels), anointing Jesus' feet as a foreshadowing of his burial, using her hair to wipe his feet. In John 13–14, Jesus wipes the feet of his disciples as he prepares them for his departure, calls them to become mature disciples who serve others in the name of Jesus, and equips them to do greater works than he himself did (John 14:12).

1. Compare the foot washing to John 12:1-6. What do you think about all of the physical touch present in these stories and many others in John's Gospel? Did you realize that the dearly loved disciple is reclining upon Jesus' chest, not next to Jesus (John 13:23-25)? Who is touching whom in each story? How would the same kinds of interactions go over in your community today? How does the Gospel's intimate touching relate to recognizing Jesus as a human being among us?

2. In biblical times, it was usually the job of a Gentile (not Jewish) slave or of a woman to wash the feet of her husband. Why does

Peter resist having his feet washed by a person considered to be his superior? What is Jesus trying to teach his disciples about power in this story? How does this relate to Jesus' proclamation in John 15:15: "I don't call you servants any longer. . . . Instead, I call you friends." Do you think of yourselves as a community of Jesus' friends or as servants submitting to a master? What difference does it make for relating to God and each other in covenant relationship?

3. In John 13:15 Jesus says, "I have given you an example: Just as I have done, you also must do." Have you ever participated in a foot washing? If so, what was it like? Does your community practice foot washing? If so, what effect does that practice have?

SIGNS OF FAITHFUL LOVE

The signs pointing to Jesus (who serves and lives for others, who brings about new birth) are visible through the intensity of personal actions, such as foot washing.

EPISODE 18

Psalms

PRAISE AND LAMENT
Bring everything to God in prayer.

Bible Readings

Day 1: Psalms 1–2; 19; 119:1-42
Day 2: Psalms 13; 22; 80; 90
Day 3: Psalms 34; 107; 116; 138
Day 4: Psalms 8; 104; 148
Day 5: Psalms 146–150
Day 6: Covenant Meditation on Psalm 139:1-6
Day 7: Group Meeting Experience with Psalm 42

Covenant Prayer

For the voiceless and oppressed

God! Hear my prayer; listen to the words of my mouth! (Psalm 54:2)

For truth-tellers and encouragers

You who are faithful to the LORD, sing praises to him; give thanks to his holy name! His anger lasts for only a second, but his favor lasts a lifetime. (Psalm 30:4-5a)

OUR LONGING FOR RELATIONSHIP

Whether life is going well or not well at all, we share our grateful praise and our desperate pleas for help with the one who loves us.

PSALMS

The Psalms mention our covenant with God at least twenty times. Psalm 25:10 assures us that "all the Lord's paths are loving and faithful for those who keep his covenant and laws." The covenant, which is confirmed in God's faithful love, allows us to bring everything to God in prayer, including prayers for help (laments), shouts of praise, and times for giving thanks concerning the things that God is doing.

Psalms is the longest book of the Bible and the most diverse in themes. Nowhere else in the scriptures is found such a varied collection of religious poetry: 150 psalms in the Hebrew canon; 151 in the ancient Greek translation (the Septuagint). The Psalter contains a remarkable array of literary forms: desperate prayers for help (or laments), ecstatic praises, songs giving thanks, songs declaring trust, and instructions for faithful living, not to overlook a wedding song and several psalms expressing regret for sin. The popular writer Anne Lamott identifies "three essential prayers" for the faithful life: Help, Thanks, and Wow (which is the title of her book). The Psalms have those covered, and much more.

Common to all the various forms of psalms is their focus on God. In the Psalms, the God who commands is also the God who sustains. The God of kings and the God of the poor, the God of judgment and the God of mercy, the God who creates and the God who redeems, God's hidden face and God's beaming countenance: All these opposites are represented in the Psalms (and elsewhere in the Bible). That's why Martin Luther regarded the Psalms as the "little Bible."

Yet, for all its variety, the Psalter consists primarily of human words directed to God or proclaimed about God in the context of worship. They are, in the broadest sense, liturgical. Many of them are used in temple worship but also in smaller, more intimate settings. Even as liturgy, the Psalms are unique for their personal tone: Some psalms are filled with anguish and despair, some burst with joy, and others exude gratitude.

Another common feature of the Psalms is their poetry. Psalmic poetry, like biblical poetry in general, has its own structure. It is filled with images and rhythms, inviting the reader to feel, sense, and imagine. As poetry, a psalm lends itself to recitation or singing, and only thereafter to interpretation. A poem must be sounded; otherwise, its oral quality is lost, its rhythm and rhyme with its repeated and pleasant combinations of sounds are missed. Such

---

A poem must be sounded; otherwise, its oral quality is lost, its rhythm and rhyme with its repeated and pleasant combinations of sounds are missed.

qualities have compelled many to compare poetry with music. It's no coincidence that many of the psalms include instructions for musical accompaniment (see, for example, the superscriptions for Pss 22; 45; 56; 60; 69; 80).

> **Optional:** *An additional video on the Psalms—which we speak aloud in worship and which tell our contemporary stories—is available for download from* **CovenantBibleStudy.com**.

As for the poetry of the Psalms, there are two defining features: parallelism and metaphor. One example illustrates both quite vividly:

> Just like a deer that craves streams of water,
> > my whole being craves you, God. (Ps 42:1)

Here the psalmist evokes the image of the deer and applies it to his (or her) whole being in the second line. The speaker's being is metaphorically identified with the thirsty deer. In the same way, streams of water are identified with God. The poet constructs this metaphor in parallel poetic lines: A deer bears a positive identification with the psalmist's whole being, as do streams with God. There is a positive, constructive relationship between the lines that advances the message, and this is called "synonymous parallelism."

The opposite of synonymous parallelism is also found frequently. Take, for example, the following two verses, each representing a two-line poetic unit:

> Some people trust in chariots, others in horses;
> > but we praise the Lord's name.
> They will collapse and fall,
> > but we will stand up straight and strong. (Ps 20:7-8)

The "but" in both verses sets up a contrast: Trust in military might is contrasted with praising "the Lord's name" in the first verse, and vanquished enemies are set apart from the victors ("we") in the second verse. The contrast reflected in each of these poetic verses is called "antithetical parallelism." Many verses in the Psalms, however, are neither "synonymous" nor "antithetical," as in Psalms 124:6 and 113:3, where the thought begun in the first line is completed in the second. However we regard the relationship between the lines of a poetic verse in Psalms, we can unlock the clue to its meaning when we understand that each poetic verse is constructed as a unit of two, and sometimes three (Ps 124:6), lines in parallel relationship to each other. In the Common English Bible, the first line of a verse unit begins at the left margin, and the second (and sometimes third) is slightly indented.

Like snowflakes, no two psalms are entirely alike. Yet many exhibit common forms or patterns. Various types of psalms can be identified, not unlike the way field biologists classify botanical species. The basic presupposition of studying the Psalms' forms or types is that any given psalm is best understood not in isolation, but in relation to psalms of similar language and structure. Among the 150 psalms of the Psalter, the following major types have been identified: complaint prayers or laments (which can be either individual or communal), hymns or praise songs, individual thanksgiving songs, songs of trust, and royal psalms. Several subtypes and mixed types have also been proposed.

The Psalter is a collection of collections of psalms. Several collections are determined by their superscriptions or titles, such as the Davidic collection (Pss 3–41; 51–71; 108–110; 138–145), the Korahite collection (Pss 42–49; 84–85; 87–88), and the Asaphite collection (Pss 50; 73–83). Each psalm within these collections bears a superscription or title that attributes the psalm to a person or people. Most prominent is David, whose name appears in nearly half of the Psalms: seventy-three, to be exact. The other "personal" collections include that of the Korahites, a guild of temple personnel; and that of Asaph, a temple singer appointed by David. These collections don't necessarily claim historical authorship. The Hebrew word for the preposition *of* in the title "A psalm of David" can also mean "for," "belonging to," or "about" David.

Other psalms bear no such attribution. Many are united by a common theme or literary distinction, such as the so-called enthronement hymns (Pss 47; 93; 95–99), pilgrimage songs (Pss 120–134), and hallelujah psalms (Pss 111–117; 146–150). The enthronement hymns celebrate God's kingship over Israel and the nations with the resounding proclamation "The Lord rules!" (Pss 93:1; 96:10; 97:1; 99:1). The pilgrimage songs (the Hebrew idiom is "songs for going up," sometimes translated "Songs of Ascents" in the NIV and NRSV) are a more diverse group and are distinguished by their unique superscription. They may have been sung by pilgrims going up to the Jerusalem temple to worship. The two groupings of hallelujah psalms include psalms for thanksgiving and praise, many of which open with the command to praise. Each of the last five psalms of the Psalter is bracketed by the command "Praise the Lord!" (*hallelujah* in Hebrew), providing a fitting conclusion to the Psalms as a whole. It is no coincidence that the Hebrew title to the book of Psalms is "Praises" (Hebrew *tehillim*).

Then there are those outlier psalms, such as Psalms 89 and 90, whose pedigree has no other precedent in the Psalter: Moses and Ethan. Psalms 72 and 127 are both ascribed to Solomon, but they are part of the Davidic collection and the pilgrimage songs, respectively. Several psalms lack superscriptions altogether; they are the "orphans" of the Psalter. They include Psalms 1–2; 10; 43; 71; 91; 104–107; 118–119; 136–137. Two, however, are simply untitled extensions of previous psalms, Psalms 10 and 43. Psalms 1 and 2, in addition, bear no superscription, perhaps because they serve as the introduction to the Psalter as a whole.

Day 1: Psalms 1–2; 19; 119:1-42
God's expectations

Although Psalms 1 and 2 are quite different in content from each other, they are linked together and placed strategically at the beginning of the Psalter. Psalm 1 has as its central focus the "Lord's Instruction" (Ps 1:2), sharing a common concern with Psalms 19 and 119, so-called Torah psalms because they, too, contain instructions. Read Psalms 19 and 119 (the longest psalm in the Psalter) to see their similarities and differences. How is God's "Instruction" portrayed in each psalm? Psalm 119 is an acrostic, in which each section begins with a subsequent letter of the Hebrew alphabet (which is illustrated in the CEB).

The second psalm, a royal psalm, features God's chosen king established on Zion (Ps 2:2*b*, 6-7). The first psalm features two antithetical characters: the wicked and the righteous. Note how both are vividly described, metaphorically and ethically, in contrasting ways. The second psalm also juxtaposes two contrasting characters: God's "anointed" king and the raging enemies that threaten him. God's decree of the king's sonship (Ps 2:7) ensures the king's victory. How are these two contrasting characters in Psalm 2 described?

Though widely divergent in content and style, these two psalms are linked together. Can you find any similarities between these psalms in terms of language and theme? For example, consider how Psalm 1 begins and how Psalm 2 ends.

What are the various contexts or situations for "happiness" according to these two psalms?

Day 2: Psalms 13; 22; 80; 90
Desperate prayer for help

The lament psalms (also called complaints, prayers for help, or petitions) constitute the majority of psalms in the Psalter, more than one-third. Indeed, they form the Psalter's "backbone." They are most frequently cast in the first-person singular voice ("I"), as in Psalms 13 and 22. Psalms 80 and 90 are examples of community laments in the plural voice ("we").

Most laments move from complaint to praise. A simple example is Psalm 13. Observe how this short psalm moves quickly from complaint (cast in the form of questions) to prayer, and from prayer to confession of trust and praise. Note also the reasons given by the speaker for why God should save him (Ps 13:3b-5).

Psalm 22, by contrast, is much more elaborate. No other psalm in the Psalter plumbs despair so deeply and scales the heights of praise so resolutely. It stretches the genre of lament as far as it can go, extending fully in both directions: complaint and praise. Read the psalm carefully, noting how it moves from complaint and despair to trust and prayer, frequently alternating back and forth, and finally leading to a glorious buildup of praise to God. Some of the images in this psalm may seem particularly familiar to you, since the authors of the Gospels knew this psalm well and used images from it to describe the suffering and death of Jesus.

Where precisely does Psalm 22 make the switch from prayer to testimony of salvation, resulting in the speaker's trust and praise? (Hint: It happens so quickly that it can easily be missed!)

Day 3: Psalms 34; 107; 116; 138
Giving thanks

Psalm 107 qualifies as the most elaborate thanksgiving psalm in the Bible. Compare it with the simpler Psalm 138. The defining mark of a thanksgiving psalm is the testimony to God's deliverance in response to prayer (see Ps 138:3, 7). Psalm 107 opens with a command to give thanks, followed by the reason or motivation for doing so, namely, God's "faithful love" (Ps 107:1b). The psalm then depicts four situations of distress.

How would you describe each of these situations? How is God's "faithful love" operative in each situation?

Each scene concludes with an exhortation, which serves as a refrain for the entire psalm: "Let them thank the Lord for his faithful love" (Ps 107:8, 15, 21, 31). In the Psalter, "faithful love" best summarizes God's nature with respect to the covenant between God and individual or community. To speak of God's "faithful love" is to acknowledge God's responsiveness to human need, particularly in times of distress (see Ps 103:8).

The final section of the psalm (Ps 107:33-43) is filled with summary statements illustrating God's grace and judgment.

Who receives God's judgment? God's grace?

The psalm appropriately concludes with the admonition to pay attention, "carefully considering the Lord's faithful love" (Ps 107:43). To consider God's love, the psalmist contends, leads naturally to thanksgiving. Psalms 34 and 116 are other excellent examples of thanksgiving psalms. Psalm 34 is also an acrostic, with each verse beginning with the next letter of the Hebrew alphabet (which is illustrated in the CEB).

Day 4: Psalms 8; 104; 148
Creation songs

Psalm 104 is a hymn that celebrates the sheer diversity of creation (Ps 104:24). It begins and ends with the command to "bless the Lord," that is, give God due praise (Ps 104:1, 35b). Most of the psalm describes God's acts in creation and God's provision of water, vegetation, food, and habitat for a variety of animals, from lions to Leviathan (elsewhere described as a monster of the deep; see Ps 74:12-14). God's "breath" (Ps 104:30) creates and renews life. For the beauty of the earth, the psalmist boldly attributes to God well-deserved joy ("rejoice . . . !") in creation (Ps 104:31b). The last verses cast the psalm as an offering of praise that God, it is hoped, will find "pleasing" (see also Ps 19:14).

One of the striking things about Psalm 104 is the place of humanity within this cosmic panorama. Compare the place of humanity in this psalm with humanity's place in Psalms 8 and 148. Are they different? In Psalm 104, human beings aren't mentioned until verse 15, and in verses 21 through 23 the only difference between humans and lions is that lions take the night shift!

How does Psalm 104:35a, with reference to the wicked, reveal the psalmist's view of humanity in creation?

Day 5: Psalms 146–150
Hallelujah!

The concluding songs of the Psalter (Pss 146–150) each open and conclude with the command "Praise the Lord!" (*hallelujah* in Hebrew). Note their differences and similarities, particularly with respect to how each psalm describes what God has done to warrant such praise. Psalm 147 may very well be the most elaborate praise psalm in the Psalter because it contains three separate hymns, each one with its own particular emphases. As is typical with songs of praise, each hymn within this psalm opens with a command to render praise to God.

The first mini-hymn (Ps 147:1-6) celebrates God's redemptive and healing activity on behalf of Israel amid the ravages of exile. In addition, the hymn celebrates God's work in numbering and naming the stars (Ps 147:4). The second hymn (Ps 145:7-11) includes God's acts of creation and provision for animals, but concludes with God's delight specifically in "the people who honor him" (Ps 147:11). The final hymn is the most intricate, given the specific focus on God's "word" and its wide range of functions (Ps 147:15-19), from controlling the seasons to delivering Israel's Instruction. Psalm 147 is a testimony to the variety of divine activities in the world and within the community.

What would cause you to say "hallelujah" today?

Day 6: Psalm 139:1-6
Covenant Meditation: Lord, you know me.

As we have learned through this week's readings, the Psalms contain many honest prayers about despair, depression, confession, doubt, anxiety, pride, humility, joy, and praise. Too often in the congregation we feel pressure to express positive, joyful, and uplifting thoughts when praying. And yet here in the Psalms, through these songs and laments, we are reminded that our covenant with God makes room for us to bring all we experience into prayer. If not to God, then to whom can we speak the fullness of the light and darkness, trust and doubt, praises and laments of our lives?

For this devotional reading, meditate on Psalm 139:1-6. We will practice prayerful listening for a verse or phrase in the text with special meaning for your life today. God wants you to listen.

Read the full text once slowly and with intention, attending to every phrase and verse. Then do this again, at the same pace. Select one verse or phrase that catches your attention in any way; don't analyze why this is. Now read this one verse or phrase slowly a few times. In an attitude of prayer ask God, "What do you want me to hear?" Try to be still for a few minutes with this question and listen.

You may hear a word from God in this quiet time—an instruction, a correction, an encouragement—and if so, receive this as a prayer for you. You might not hear anything particular from this reading now, but it may stay with you until another time of listening to God. Just sitting still and silent with these words is true prayer.

After your time of listening is complete, give God thanks for this time.

Group Meeting Experience

Psalm 42 | Like a deer that craves streams of water

During this week with the Psalms, we learned about parallelism in poetry and how thinking or communicating with images (metaphor) is helpful when expressing our deepest yearnings and frustrations to God.

1. In certain psalms, a single image bears a wealth of metaphorical associations. Discuss how the imagery of water is used metaphorically, particularly in the first seven verses of Psalm 42.

2. What is repeated that constitutes the psalm's refrain? Who is addressed in the refrain?

3. How would you describe the mood of the speaker? Can you detect shifts in the speaker's emotional disposition? What seems to cause such shifts?

4. What is the relationship between Psalms 42 and 43? Could they constitute one psalm together? Cite evidence one way or the other, taking into consideration repeated words and phrases, as well as the usual form of the lament.

SIGNS OF FAITHFUL LOVE

While Covenant people need to reach and touch the Lord, there are moments when the Lord reaches for us in faithful love. The Psalms shout our mutual, loyal love in deep and trusted words that are spoken, sung, screamed, and cried.

EPISODE 19

Job

TRAGEDY
God's role in human suffering

Bible Readings

Day 1: Job 1–2
Day 2: Job 3; 9; 19; 31
Day 3: Job 4–5; 8; 11
Day 4: Job 38–41
Day 5: Job 42; reread Job 1–2
Day 6: Covenant Meditation on Job 2
Day 7: Group Meeting Experience with Job 42:7-17

Covenant Prayer

For those who feel abandoned by God

Come back to me, Lord! Deliver me! Save me for the sake of your faithful love! (Psalm 6:4)

For faith communities and faithful friends

Come back to us, Lord! Please, quick! Have some compassion for your servants! . . . Let the kindness of the Lord our God be over us. Make the work of our hands last. Make the work of our hands last! (Psalm 90:13, 17)

OUR LONGING FOR RELATIONSHIP

When life gets tough, and loss or suffering is all around, you ask, "Why?" You ask for help. You need comfort. You can't explain why, and your friends can't explain the loss.

JOB

The book of Job begins by presenting a single character's experience of personal tragedy. First, a narrator tells of the reversal of Job's circumstances and fortunes, which includes the loss of his family, his prosperity, and his health. Then a range of voices—including Job's friends, God, and the narrator's own voice—debate the connection between personal experience and religious tradition. Can one draw conclusions or formulate doctrine about who God is based on a single person's experience? How should humans respond to God based on Job's experience? In trying to understand why tragedy occurs, should you favor your immediate experience, or can you gain a mature peace with human suffering by looking at a long tradition of reflection about God's ways with the world?

The book of Proverbs is a book like Job that contains the wisdom of Israel's sages. Proverbs teaches that if one looks closely enough at the structures of creation, we will find God's deep commitment to order, which is embedded within the universe. By contrast with Proverbs, the book of Job raises the possibility that one will find no divine commitment to order or justice. Rather, if one looks at God through the experiences of the character Job, we seem to encounter a God who does what God pleases and who seems unconcerned with justice for Job. If we read with Job, we find the God of a nightmare who permits and imposes excruciating tests of righteousness on a good and righteous person. Job uses the lens of personal tragedy, rather than that of doctrine, tradition, or orthodoxy, to inspect God's intent for the world. When this lens is held up to God, as Virginia Woolf once said, "God does not come off well."

And yet, Job's perspective in the dialogue isn't the only one the reader encounters in the book. Job's view is rooted firmly, even stubbornly, in his own experience of terrible tragedy and in his own conviction that the faithful ("the righteous" in the language of the Old Testament) should be rewarded, rather than tested or afflicted. Job never mentions the great biblical covenants describing the responsibilities of God and people to each other, but his protests clearly assume the theology of rewards and punishments present in the biblical covenant at Mount Sinai. Alongside Job's view, the author(s) present other theological worldviews, including those represented by the prose story, Job's three friends, the wisdom poem (Job 28), Elihu the fourth friend (Job 32–37), as well as the literary character God (Job 38–41).

Through the voices of these different characters, the book raises and debates a stunningly wide range of questions, including the motivation for piety, the meaning of suffering, the nature of God, the place of justice in the world, and the relationship of order and chaos in God's design of creation.

Often, when readers engage the book, from start to finish they find it to be overwhelming, confusing, or even nonsensical at times. Jerome (a Christian scholar from the 300s CE) said that the book of Job is like an eel, "for if you close your hand to hold an eel, the more you squeeze it, the sooner it escapes." But the fact that the book doesn't speak with one voice may point to its purpose. The writer(s) is probably a skeptic, not only when it comes to tradition and orthodoxy, but also in the face of any single proposal of truth. The swirling perspectives and opposing views communicate that tragedy can't be explained easily or simply, and definitely not by one voice. When the innocent suffer, there are a variety of ways to make sense of that suffering, but each of the explanations we can give and perspectives we can offer ultimately fails to win the day. Though the book undermines theological certitude, the book also assumes that God hasn't completely abandoned the world to its own problems and evils and that God is in relationship with us, involved in our human suffering.

The book implicitly claims that humans are able to survive and endure suffering because they try to make sense of it. By trying to make sense of it, we engage in the process of bringing some order to the chaos of tragedy. Perhaps best of all, however, the book gives readers permission to *not* make sense of suffering. While we are encouraged to ask the questions and formulate ideas and arguments, the book's voices, sometimes a choir and sometimes a noisy crowd, ultimately assure us that while we may formulate answers to tough theological questions about pain and suffering, they won't ever be the final answers.

It is very difficult to identify the historical setting that produced Job. It contains only a handful of historical clues (for example, the Chaldeans in Job 1:17). The story is set in the far-off and non-Israelite land of Uz and features characters with non-Israelite names. The prose narrative, in particular, gives the impression that the story is one from ages past. For linguistic reasons, most scholars agree on a Persian-period date for the book (600–400 BCE), at some point after the Israelites were dispersed into exile. Since the book of Job deals with the universal experience of tragedy, its precise historical setting is less important than the broad issues it engages.

God hasn't completely abandoned the world to its own problems and evils, and God is in relationship with us, involved in our human suffering.

Some scholars think that the prose tale (Job 1–2; 42:11-17) existed and circulated independently as a folktale. Later, a scribe (or scribes), a member of the learned elite in Jerusalem, possibly added the dialogue (Job 3–31), including the wisdom poem (Job 28) and the divine speeches (Job 38–41), as a way to articulate implicit questions raised by the prose tale. A third stage may have occurred when a still-later reader who found the friends' defense of traditional theological views lacking added the speeches of Elihu to the book in order to provide a more compelling, orthodox response to Job's suffering. But most readers of Job don't worry about how the book was edited and favor looking at the ways the various speakers interact, anticipate, contend with, or undermine each other in the book.

The dialogue between Job and his friends (Job 3–27) is often compared to a text from Mesopotamia, the "Babylonian Theodicy," which features a conversation between two friends—one who is experiencing suffering and one who offers traditional theological advice as a means to reflect on the meaning of suffering.

Day 1: Job 1–2
Job's story

The story in Job 1–2 is striking because it begins by depicting God as allowing, and even condoning, the imposition of tremendous suffering—emotional and physical—on an innocent individual. Job is described not merely as innocent but as "honest, a person of absolute integrity; he feared God and avoided evil" (Job 1:1, 8; 2:3). The question about Job's character is posed by the Adversary (Hebrew *satan*), who here is one of the divine beings in the heavenly court (but not the prince of evil from the New Testament). While the Adversary questions the motivation underlying Job's righteous behaviors, both God and the narrator affirm the perfection of Job's character. And yet, God allows his destruction as a means to test that character. In Job 1–2, Job's response to his suffering is quite different from what we will find in the dialogue that follows. In the prose story, Job is an example of traditional piety, accepting his suffering without complaint (Job 1:20-21; 2:10). According to the prologue, tragedy is the result of divine testing, and Job's submission to God's will is an example of the proper response.

And yet, when you read the story closely, attending to the details of this tale, you may find that the story begins to raise theological questions of a more skeptical nature for you.

Do you think that God tests us with suffering?

Day 2: Job 3; 9; 19; 31
Job's response

The accusations Job levels at God in the course of his speeches are among the most theologically daring statements in the Old Testament. His characterization of God as one who intentionally distorts justice and willfully attacks innocents is radical, and at times even horrifying (Job 6:4; 9:22-24; 16:9-14; 19:8-12).

While other texts in the Old Testament indict God for human suffering, they sometimes temper their accusations or justify divine anger by referring to human sin (Pss 32:5; 38:18; 41:4; Lam 3:40-42) and seek to pacify God's anger with pleas for mercy. But Job insists in the speeches that divine acts of violence and harassment against him are arbitrary and erratic, and he demands justice from God. Other Old Testament texts suggest that human suffering occurs because God is sleeping or not paying attention; therefore, human enemies are free to oppress innocent people (Ps 28:1-2). Job, by contrast, depicts God as one who pays particular attention to faithful people, watching them and waiting for them to sin so that God can torment them. Job begs God, not to see him and save him, but rather to look away from him and leave him alone (Job 7:16-21).

For Job in the speeches, the cause of his personal tragedy is God. Therefore, in contrast to the laments in the book of Psalms, which often complain about "the enemies" and their relentless harassment of the faithful, Job resists introducing a third party who might shoulder some of the blame for his suffering. In fact, Job's hope persists not in the possibility that God will intervene and redeem him, but in the desire that some third party (for example, "a mediator") might intercede on Job's behalf and restrain God from tormenting Job (Job 9:33-35).

Have you ever yelled at God? Or demanded an explanation for pain and suffering? What was the cause of your frustration?

Day 3: Job 4–5; 8; 11
The friends' arguments

Job's friends—Eliphaz, Bildad, and Zophar—maintain that God has reasons for imposing suffering on people that we can't always understand at first. They propose that God may be trying to draw Job closer into relationship with God. They urge Job to turn back to God by turning away from sin. In the face of Job's personal and theological world falling to pieces, they counsel Job to remember the tenets of their common faith, to lend order to the chaos of his suffering with the theological convictions of their common tradition. For the friends, tragedy happens for a reason: human sin and frailty (Job 4:7-8). We should accept suffering as an opportunity to reflect on our weaknesses. We should turn away from sin to draw nearer to God and to become more faithful.

Although the friends' views are rarely taken seriously when we sympathize with Job, and in spite of the friends' bluntness, they may have something theologically significant to offer to the dialogue when encountering the problem and causes of pain. The friends express views held by many people of faith, especially when thinking that the suffering person is at fault or when wondering whether a particular person deserves pain as a punishment.

Do you think that some pain and suffering is deserved?

Day 4: Job 38–41
God's speeches from the whirlwind

How do God's speeches answer the questions and issues Job raises in the dialogue? After the dialogue's focus on the expectation for justice and the reason for human suffering, God suddenly appears and speaks not about justice (at least on the surface), but about creation. A related question raised by God's speeches has to do with the speeches' tone. Some readers experience God as a bully, badgering the suffering Job and bragging about God's handiwork in creation. Therefore, they ask, "Is the creation theme a means to change the subject?" Do these speeches aim to distract readers from

God's behavior in the prologue? The two portrayals of God, in the prologue and in the divine speeches, are quite different. It is fruitful to explore the differences as well as the similarities between the two. Other readers, perhaps weary of Job's focus on his suffering, cheer the words from God, claiming that they rightly set Job straight and remind him that the world wasn't created solely with his comfort in mind. Either way, in the view presented by the voice of God, human tragedy isn't personal; it is the cost of living in a world in which order and chaos both have a place.

Are tragedy and suffering simply expected and inevitable in an imperfect universe?

Day 5: Job 42; reread Job 1–2
Job's response to God and the epilogue

Job's response to God in Job 42:1-6 is notable for its ambiguity. Issues with the Hebrew are often neatly cleaned up in English translations, but Job's final words in the book are open-ended. Job 42:6, the key to Job's response to God's speeches, has usually been translated in the tradition of the King James Version: "Therefore I despise myself, and repent in dust and ashes" (NRSV, NIV). This suggests that Job gives up his case against God because he finally recognizes his sin and the inaccuracy of his claims against God. But in the Hebrew text, the verb *despise* has no object (the word *myself* doesn't actually occur in Hebrew), and *despise* may also be translated "relent" or "reject." Furthermore, the verb rendered as *repent* may be translated "find comfort" or "be consoled." Thus Job's response may be translated as it is in the Common English Bible: "Therefore, I relent and find comfort on dust and ashes." Job stops arguing not because he has changed his heart and mind, but because he recognizes he is merely a limited human being—and he makes peace with that. Readers can't know for certain if Job's words indicate heartfelt satisfaction with what God has said or if they are uttered sarcastically or with resignation.

Whereas Job 42:1-6 is the conclusion to the conversation with God that precedes it, the epilogue in Job 42:7-17 returns to the naive style of the prologue. This ending to Job is one of the most difficult aspects of the book. In the wake of the book's complex presentation of the issues and questions related to innocent suffering, many readers express dissatisfaction with Job's ending because it negates what the book appears to teach—in Job's argument and in God's speeches—that there is no connection between tragedy and the pious avoidance of sin. The return of Job's possessions and the granting of a new family appear to be a reward for Job's speaking rightly about God (Job 42:7). Readers may feel as though they are back where they started with a theology of rewards and punishments that always works. And yet, if the book's aim is to frustrate attempts to provide a single explanation for innocent suffering, the epilogue succeeds by questioning the explanation for tragedy in the divine speeches. If readers accept the speeches from God (Job 38–41) about suffering, and if readers dismiss the prologue's view as overly simple or naive, the epilogue opens up the conversation again.

After something terrible happens to a person, what do you tell that person? What spiritual wisdom about God do you try to convey?

Day 6: Job 2

Covenant Meditation: What do you say to a friend in pain?

Without the details of Job's tragic loss, there is no story here for us. In the first two chapters of Job, everything of value to him—children, wealth, honor—is destroyed through tragedy until he has nothing to show for his life but sores and ashes. Our devotional meditation for this week invites you to become more attuned to Job's experience of tragedy, reading scripture with your imagination.

This week's theme, "Tragedy," is viewed through the complex and varied perspectives of the book of Job. In the first chapter we witness the orchestrated, tragic destruction of all that is valued by one righteous, God-fearing man. But what especially illumines Job's losses for us is that the God of the covenant not only refuses to prevent the pending tragedies, but also knowingly permits them to occur.

In the first chapter Job is presented as an "honest" man, "a person of absolute integrity" (Job 1:1) and endowed with sons and daughters, servants and livestock such that "he was greater than all the people of the east" (Job 1:3). We also read that Job is faithful to God before tragedy strikes and after losing everything he loves. Yet, even then, his trials are not over.

Read Job 2:1-13. As you do, try to imagine that you are Job's close friend, sitting with him as he grieves the news of his losses. Pay particular attention to verses 2 through 13. How do you feel as you imagine being there? From where you sit, what do you hear, see, taste, smell, or touch in this scene? What are you talking about with your friend? What does Job look like before the sores appear; how does his appearance change? How do you react when his skin suddenly breaks out with lesions all over his body? What do you want to do? How do you react to what Job's wife says to him? Imagine how she appears in her own grief as the other three friends show up to console Job. Pay attention to the feelings this reading brings up for you about your own experience of tragedy or that of a friend. Reflect on any insight or question that comes to you through this reading. Release all of this to God in prayer.

Group Meeting Experience

Job 42:7-17 | *Double for his trouble?*

In the final scene of Job, the author tries to tie up loose threads from the book and returns to the losses named in the opening prologue (Job 1–2). The epilogue returns the reader to the world of the prologue, and yet, as we have seen, there are differences. What is the significance of these differences? Are we back where we started? Or does the epilogue move the conversation about tragedy in a new direction?

1. God indicates in the epilogue that Job has spoken what is right about God (Job 42:7), which is not what God says in the poetic speech at Job 38:2; there Job speaks "words lacking knowledge." What has Job said that is "right"? And what have the friends said that is "wrong"?

2. Read Exodus 22:4-9 and then reflect on what it means if "the Lord doubled all Job's earlier possessions" (Job 42:10). Is God compensating Job out of regret for allowing the suffering? Or is God merely showing compassion for what Job has suffered? Also discuss the narrator's judgment that Job's family "comforted and consoled him concerning all the disaster the Lord had brought on him" (Job 42:11).

3. How do you explain God's role in the murder of Job's children in the prologue, along with the narrator's report in Job 42 that Job has ten new children (three daughters and seven sons, just as before in Job 1:2)?

4. The epilogue returns the reader to the world of the prologue, and yet the Adversary is absent from the scene. Why? And what does his absence in the epilogue tell us about his purpose in the prologue?

5. There are tensions between the "patient Job" in the narrative of the prologue/epilogue and the angry, "outspoken Job" in the poetic sections in between. Following a proliferation of words in the dialogue, Job doesn't speak in the epilogue. In what ways do the "Jobs" of the various portions of the book complement and contrast with each other? In the same way, there is tension between the depiction of God in the narrative and in the divine speeches. Compare and contrast these portrayals of God and discuss whether there are multiple views about God's role in the book.

6. Which of the voices in the book of Job, or combination of voices, provides for you the most satisfying response to the crisis of undeserved suffering? Why do you resonate with this voice in the book of Job?

SIGNS OF FAITHFUL LOVE

When suffering deep pain and loss, it is acceptable to tell God how you feel and why God's promises are broken. If you are yelling at God, at least you know God is present, and often that is enough.

EPISODE 20

Jeremiah, Lamentations, Ezekiel

CRISIS AND STARTING OVER
When one covenant seems to end, start over again.

Bible Readings

Day 1: Jeremiah 1–4
Day 2: Jeremiah 27–29
Day 3: Jeremiah 16; 18–20
Day 4: Lamentations 1–2; 5
Day 5: Ezekiel 34–37
Day 6: Covenant Meditation on Lamentations 3:1-24
Day 7: Group Meeting Experience with Jeremiah 31:15-34

Covenant Prayer

For children in foster care and orphanages; for youth who are incarcerated or banished from home; for all who are homeless for the first time in their lives

Why do you stand so far away, LORD, hiding yourself in troubling times? (Psalm 10:1)

For all who work in halfway houses, orphanages, and juvenile detention centers; for all who serve in shelters for refugees, domestic abuse victims, and runaway youth

I give you a new commandment: Love each other. Just as I have loved you, so you also must love each other. (John 13:34)

OUR LONGING FOR RELATIONSHIP

When things are going wrong in life (such as loss of income, loved ones, or status), relationships become fragile, and it seems like our covenant with God is broken beyond repair.

HISTORICAL CONTEXT

A crisis links the three biblical books that are the focus of this episode: Jeremiah, Ezekiel, and Lamentations. They are each a response to Babylon's attack and defeat of Judah in the early sixth century BCE.

Ever since the ninth century BCE, the northern kingdom (Israel) and the southern kingdom (Judah) had been strongly affected by international affairs. They, along with other small nations in the area of Syria-Palestine, were vulnerable to the much more powerful nations of Egypt, Assyria, and then Babylon. Their leaders always needed to decide whether to cooperate with these superpowers or to assert independence from them.

After dominating the area for several decades, Assyrian power was on the decline in the late seventh century BCE. Judah, under King Josiah, underwent religious reforms and tried to strengthen its territory. Soon afterward, Egypt and Babylon engaged in ongoing conflict, with Judah caught in the middle. While the Babylonian army was reorganizing, Judah decided to revolt. Babylon responded by mounting a military campaign against it. In 597 BCE, in what is called the first deportation, the Babylonians entered Jerusalem, raided the temple, and forced into exile the most important citizens in Jerusalem. The Babylonians installed a new king, Zedekiah, who submitted with humility for several years, but then he, too, decided to rebel. Babylon quickly responded by attacking again, destroying many of the cities in the land of Judah and putting Jerusalem under siege. Jerusalem withstood the siege for almost two years, but the city was finally captured and destroyed in 587 BCE. Much of the population that had survived was exiled to Babylon (the second deportation). A description of these events is found in 2 Kings 22–25.

The people were rocked by the violence and the trauma of these horrific events. They were left wondering why all of these things had happened. How could God let Judah—God's own nation—be destroyed? Hadn't God promised to always protect the temple and the city of Jerusalem? Didn't God care that the people were suffering so acutely? Did these events prove that their covenant with God had been broken beyond repair? The books of Jeremiah, Ezekiel, and Lamentations grapple with these sorts of questions.

JEREMIAH

Jeremiah was a member of a minor priestly family in Anathoth, a small village a few miles outside Jerusalem. His prophetic ministry was exceptionally long, beginning in 627 BCE and spanning some forty years. Throughout his career, Jeremiah preached in Jerusalem. After the fall of the city, he stayed there until he was forced to escape to Egypt. The organization of the book of Jeremiah is complex, and it includes several types of prophetic literature. In addition, the book appears to have undergone significant editing over time.

The book emphasizes the covenant relationship between God and the people. Jeremiah looks back to the covenant established by Moses, whose commandments make up the Torah, the Instruction for Israel (for example, Exod 19–31). This covenant is conditional: It is based on the people faithfully following its instructions. Jeremiah claims that the people are breaking it with their disobedience. Israel needs to turn away from their unfaithfulness in order to renew their relationship with God. Throughout the book we see the grief and anguish experienced by the prophet, the people, and even God. Jeremiah urges the people to find their security not in the temple, but in returning to their ancestral faith.

EZEKIEL

Ezekiel also prophesied during the time of the destruction, but he was most likely of a younger generation than Jeremiah, perhaps in his thirties. He was one of the prominent citizens who were taken in the first deportation to Babylon. He lived there for a few years before receiving the call to become a prophet in 593 BCE, and he continued preaching for roughly twenty more years. Like Jeremiah, Ezekiel was a priest, possibly a member of the powerful priestly family who served the temple in Jerusalem. Though he lived far away, he seemed to have a thorough knowledge of the situation there.

The book begins with a striking vision of God in a chariot. God is no longer tied down to Jerusalem but comes to be with the exiles! As we might expect from a priest, Ezekiel stresses God's holiness. The people's sinfulness shows their impurity and therefore separates them from God. The prophet is especially concerned for the temple, and his answer for the crisis of the temple's destruction is that God will build a new and better one. The book is a challenge to read, as it can seem rather strange.

The prophet describes odd visions and speaks of performing dramatic signs, being in trances, struck speechless, and carried away by a spirit. The book is well-organized, however, and the language is sophisticated. It seems that Ezekiel wrote rather than spoke many of his prophecies.

LAMENTATIONS

The book of Lamentations provides the perspective of the people who experienced the destruction and fall of Jerusalem. It's a firsthand witness to the hardship and pain that resulted from this event. The book is a series of five poems that present the viewpoints of various figures, including the community, an individual survivor, the poet, and the city itself. The poetry includes elements of biblical lament psalms, funeral songs, and city lamentations, all forms of speech that are known from ancient Near Eastern literature. The speakers tell of the horrors the city has experienced and the immense suffering of its inhabitants. They cry out for God to see their pain and to show mercy, but there is no response. God's silence is the book's main theological issue. The images in Lamentations are violent, haunting, tragic, and heartbreaking. It's hard not to turn our eyes away. Yet this biblical book helps us to imagine what it must have been like for the Israelites to experience the Babylonian attack, siege, and conquest.

These three biblical books react to the crisis of the destruction of Jerusalem from distinct perspectives:

1. a prophet in the city who is eventually exiled to Egypt (Jeremiah);

2. a prophet who has already been exiled to Babylon (Ezekiel); and

3. the city residents themselves (Lamentations).

They show us that there are many ways to respond to tragedy. Yet there are some common perspectives among them. Both Jeremiah and Ezekiel prophesy judgment as punishment for a sinful people before the fall of Jerusalem, but afterward they speak of hope and renewal. Though hope is hard to find in the midst of raw suffering, the speakers in Lamentations still continue to pray to God, to yearn for a relationship with God, and to anticipate an answer. The vantage points of these three books represent the geographical situation of diaspora that will emerge—many people in Babylon, some people in Egypt, and some people still in the land of Judah. In the diaspora, Israel will face the task of starting over and finding their new identity as the people of God. The writings of Jeremiah, Ezekiel, and Lamentations open the way to that new beginning.

Day 1: Jeremiah 1–4
Jeremiah's call and Judah's disregard of the covenant

Our first selection is the opening chapters of the book of Jeremiah. Many prophets and leaders in the Old Testament receive a call from God, and Jeremiah's call to prophesy is in the form of a dialogue (Jer 1). It was planned even before Jeremiah was born! God will transform the prophet's actual speech, putting words in his mouth. What God wants Jeremiah to say will be a message that's both difficult and hopeful, including both destruction and rebuilding. Jeremiah's call not only gives a beginning point to his ministry, but also proves that he is a true and authentic prophet.

What does Jeremiah's call and commissioning suggest about the challenge of being a prophet? In what ways does God promise to help and protect him?

Jeremiah 2–3 focuses on Israel's unfaithfulness, as do Hosea 1–3 and Ezekiel 16 and 23. Like Hosea and Ezekiel, Jeremiah uses the metaphor of a marriage to bring home his point. God's covenant with Israel is like a marriage covenant. The wife, Israel, however, has been unfaithful, has broken the covenant bond, and thus deserves punishment.

The crisis is at hand (Jer 4). In terrifying images, Jeremiah describes the disaster that's coming. An enemy who invades from the north, the direction from which Babylonian armies approach Jerusalem, is a common theme in the book. Jeremiah continues to call the people to see the very real danger of their wrong behavior, trying to convince them to return to God before it's too late.

In contemporary faith communities, whom would we say is "called"? Are there any similarities between their tasks and what Jeremiah is being charged to do?

How does the passage reflect historical marriage customs in which the husband had authority over the wife? Is it troubling to compare religious disobedience to a wife's marital infidelity?

Day 2: Jeremiah 27–29
Living under Babylonian rule

In this passage, Jeremiah speaks to two audiences: the people still in Jerusalem and the exiles who have already been taken to Babylon. In so doing, he clashes with two of the more popular prophets of the day, Hananiah and Shemaiah. Jeremiah's message in both situations is surely not what the listeners were expecting—or wanting—to hear.

Jeremiah wears a yoke to symbolize that Jerusalem's citizens are to submit to the rule, the "yoke," of Babylon (Jer 27–28). He tells the people it's God's will that Babylon, their powerful enemy, will defeat them. They aren't to resist, but are to surrender.

In a letter to the exiles in Babylon, Jeremiah's message is also that they accept their fate (Jer 29). Though God will eventually bring the people back home, it won't be in their lifetimes. The exiles need to start over and make new lives for themselves there—build houses, have families, and even pray for the good of their new neighbors.

Both of these messages confirm divine sovereignty, God's rule over creation. It is God who decides what is right in any given situation, even if it's the victory of a cruel tyrant. Jeremiah's message reminds us that we often need to take a broad view of what God might be doing in the world.

What do you think about Jeremiah's view that God takes the side of a violent empire to punish Jerusalem for its unfaithfulness? What do we do when God's word to us isn't what we want to hear? How can we get to a place of accepting it?

Day 3: Jeremiah 16; 18–20
Jeremiah's lament for himself and for his people

This reading gives insight into how difficult the prophet's life must have been. The book of Jeremiah is unique among the prophetic works in the degree to which it gives us glimpses into the interior emotional life of a prophet.

Jeremiah performs several signs during his ministry, and we see two of them in this passage. In both of them the prophet uses pottery to make his point about God's freedom to do as God chooses in this crisis situation. Just as people can break and remold pots, so God can do these things to Israel if God is displeased. These are images of a people with their covenant broken beyond repair.

In Jeremiah's cries for help, what is the prophet upset about? Does he have reason to accuse God of enticing and overpowering him?

Jeremiah sacrifices a great deal. He isn't allowed to marry or have a family in order to emphasize that destruction is coming. People plot against him and bring false charges. He's arrested and put in jail. Jeremiah's laments show the high emotional price of serving God and may be the most moving part of the entire book. These poems are much like the laments (cries for help) in the book of Psalms. Jeremiah protests his situation, accuses God, demands revenge, and at his lowest point, questions why he was even born. These details of his personal life show the struggle and the suffering required when preaching God's word.

How can we reconcile the severity of God's punishment in this passage with what we believe about God's love and mercy? Is it uncomfortable to think that God can break the people like a jug?

Day 4: Lamentations 1–2; 5
The people's call for help

The entire book of Lamentations shows the people in full crisis mode. This reading includes three of the five chapters of the book. These texts describe the collapse of society on many levels.

In Lamentations 1 and 2, the city of Jerusalem is imagined as a person, Daughter Zion. (Zion is another name for Jerusalem.) "Is there any suffering like the suffering inflicted on me?" she asks (Lam 1:12). Because it's presented as though it were happening to an actual woman, the destruction of the city seems more immediate and more emotional. These chapters include repeated images of violence and shame. All the inhabitants of the city alike are harmed—young and old, women and men.

Lamentations 5 describes the experience of the people living in their occupied land, under the control of the Babylonians. For those lucky enough to have survived, daily life is filled with numerous difficulties, and even dangers.

Again and again throughout this passage, the people call out to God to see what's happening to them. Surely their suffering is too great to bear! Yet the poet repeats that no help ever arrives, from God or from their neighbors. There's no one to comfort the people and no hopeful resolution to their wretched circumstances.

Think of cities or lands in recent years that have experienced widespread destruction. How are the experiences of their inhabitants similar to those of the inhabitants of Jerusalem?

Day 5: Ezekiel 34–37
Ezekiel's visions of transformation; a new covenant

Our single reading from the prophet Ezekiel is addressed to his contemporaries in exile in Babylon. The passage begins right after the news of Jerusalem's destruction reaches Ezekiel and the exiles (Ezek 33:21-22). This is a turning point in the book, where the prophet's message turns from warning to hope.

Ezekiel here uses images and metaphors to portray Israel's transformation. Several are contrasted with each other: for example, good sheep and bad sheep; the mountains of Israel and Mount Seir in the nation of Edom; and a new heart and a heart of stone. Two metaphors of transformation especially stand out. One is the image of God as Israel's shepherd (Ezek 34). We see the image of the good shepherd who lovingly cares for the sheep, God's people, elsewhere in the Old Testament (most famously in Ps 23) and in the New Testament (Jesus as the good shepherd; John 10:1-18). The image of dry bones is also especially powerful (Ezek 37). The people in exile felt as dead as old bones, picked clean by their predators and bleached dry in the desert sun.

The people in exile felt as dead as old bones, picked clean by their predators and bleached dry in the desert sun.

It's important to recognize that God is the one who brings about Israel's transformation. It's God who gathers the sheep (Ezek 34:11-16). It's God who breathes new life into their dead bones (Ezek 37:5-10). It's only because of God's honor, God's holiness, that Israel will be redeemed, and not because of any actions on Israel's part.

Ezekiel sees not an end to the people of Israel, but a new beginning. What seems impossible at this point can become possible. The prophet reports that the scattered people can come together once more, the temple can be rebuilt, and the land can become fertile again. The covenant between God and the people can be renewed (Ezek 34:25; 37:26).

*How does Ezekiel imagine the natural world—
animals, plants, land—in his vision for a new future?
How is the healing and renewal of the people
connected to the environment?*

Day 6: Lamentations 3:1-24
Covenant Meditation: Living with crisis

Crisis, personal or communal, can strip us down to our most vulnerable, raw, and honest selves. Crisis can peel away any facade about being in control of our lives. Often our first response to crisis is to plant our feet more deeply into the ground in order to stay upright and then to get a stranglehold on what we think will save us. But no matter how strong our hold may seem, crisis by its very nature undoes something in and around us. Crisis peels life down to a layer of vulnerability that we thought we had skillfully covered up or, at the very least, managed well.

So when crisis strikes, we are rarely at ease speaking about our fear, despair, or hopelessness—not with each other, and not even with God. We seldom practice the language of despair and lament because, somewhere along faith's way, the message was clear that to do so shows a lack of faith. Yet our readings this week counter this message and instead provide us with some of the most raw, honest crisis language "spoken" and preserved by God's children. Therefore, our spiritual reading practice for this week invites us and asks us to rehearse, through prayer, the crisis language of lament. Today we will pray the scriptures by joining with a member of the community who is suffering, grieving, and feeling so hopeless that even God seems uninterested and removed.

To prepare for the reading, locate Lamentations 3:1-24. Before reading this text, try to set aside any judgment about the content of this prayer, about whether or not you would pray these words. This prayer may not name your beliefs about God or God's ways. Instead, approach this lament with anticipation of giving voice to a sister or brother who is living in the midst of life-wrenching crisis.

Now, silently or aloud, read the verses slowly, attending to the emotions that arise with each image and phrase. Resist judgment about the prayer, but receive it with compassion and acceptance for the one who first prayed these words.

When the reading is completed, offer a brief prayer for all who live in crisis and are calling out to God for help.

Group Meeting Experience

Jeremiah 31:15-34 | *The new covenant*

In this speech, Jeremiah describes God's new covenant with the people as the basis for a new start after their deepest crisis. As Ezekiel also does, Jeremiah focuses on the people's new heart, that is, the new direction of their lives (Jer 31:33; Ezek 36:26-27). (If time permits, read all of Jer 31. It contains a beautiful expression of God's faithful love for Israel.)

1. Who is Rachel, one of Israel's ancestors? Why was she so important? How is Rachel being used as a symbol in this passage? What group is suggested by the reference to "her children"?

2. What will healing and restoration look like? How is this a new creation? How will the people be different after the restoration?

3. What is God doing in this passage? What are God's emotions? Do they surprise you at all?

4. How does the language about building and planting echo that in Jeremiah's original call to prophesy (Jer 1:10)? Do the images of fertility enhance the prophet's message?

5. How do we understand the Instructions that are engraved on the people's hearts? How is the "new covenant" different from the previous covenant?

SIGNS OF FAITHFUL LOVE

Covenant people may seem abandoned and broken beyond repair, but they hope again when their trust in God is restored through new relationships and even through a new covenant.

EPISODE 21

Isaiah 40-66

Exile and Renewal
The risk of being in charge

Bible Readings

Day 1: Isaiah 40–43
Day 2: Isaiah 49:1–52:12
Day 3: Isaiah 52:13–55:13
Day 4: Isaiah 56:1-8; 58–61
Day 5: Isaiah 63:7–66:24
Day 6: Covenant Meditation on Isaiah 43:1-7
Day 7: Group Meeting Experience with Isaiah 40:12-31

Covenant Prayer

For those uprooted from their home for any reason

I know the plans I have in mind for you, declares the Lord; they are plans for peace, not disaster, to give you a future filled with hope. (Jeremiah 29:11)

For poets, artists, writers, and dancers who bear the beauty of God's hope to others

Don't fear, because I am with you; don't be afraid, for I am your God. I will strengthen you, I will surely help you; I will hold you with my righteous strong hand. (Isaiah 41:10)

OUR LONGING FOR RELATIONSHIP

When faith becomes acceptable to the majority, or when we are in charge and our experience of God becomes mainstream, our challenge is to avoid apathy.

ISAIAH 40-66

The readings this week come from the second half of the book of Isaiah. Most Prophetic Books in the Bible are collections of speeches, many from the prophet after whom the book is named, but many also from followers of this prophet who have appended their speeches to those of their revered predecessor. Most of the speeches in the first half of Isaiah, which were studied in Episode 16, were composed by Isaiah of Jerusalem, who was active around 735–700 BCE.

The speeches in the second half of the book, Isaiah 40–66, which are now attached to the prophecies of Isaiah of Jerusalem, come from a very different time. They were composed by followers of Isaiah during the exile and afterward, beginning around 540 BCE, a generation after Jeremiah and Ezekiel. No one knows exactly when or how these various prophecies were joined into a single book. The most important thread binding them is their shared concern for Jerusalem and its relationship to God.

Of the four eighth-century prophets (Amos, Hosea, Micah, and Isaiah), Isaiah was the only Jerusalem resident. During his time, the rest of Judah and Israel were destroyed by the Assyrian Empire, and Jerusalem itself was nearly destroyed. Isaiah 39 (compare 2 Kgs 20) anticipates Jerusalem's eventual invasion not by Assyria in the eighth century, but by the next great empire, Babylon, in the sixth century.

The destruction of Jerusalem and of Solomon's temple by Babylon in 587 BCE is described in 2 Kings 25. The tragedy is vividly remembered in Jeremiah, Ezekiel, Lamentations, and in several psalms. Some Judeans were exiled to Babylon, and some took refuge elsewhere, but most were left destitute in Judah. For this reason, some scholars call this period the "exile," while others think of it as the period without the temple, which seems appropriate for the majority of people who didn't leave after Jerusalem's fall.

Not much is known directly about conditions of any Judean group in this period. This silence may indicate the unspeakable extent of the trauma. Instead of dwelling on the present, writers during this time reconstructed the deep past from which Judah's identity had emerged and, it was hoped, would reemerge. A great deal of the Bible's formation comes from this time. Rather than being destroyed, scripture as we know it was preserved, shaped, and reborn in tragedy and suffering.

See Maps 8, 10, and 12 showing the Assyrian, Babylonian, and Persian Empires in the CEB Study Bible.

About a generation after Jerusalem's destruction, when Babylon's power was waning, Persia's King Cyrus began to claim dominance. When he captured and entered Babylon itself, he decreed leniency toward captive nations, including the Judean captives there. According to Ezra 1:1-4 and 2 Chronicles 36:22-23, Judeans in Babylon were encouraged by Cyrus to return home and rebuild their city and temple.

ISAIAH 40–55: PROPHET OF THE EXILE

Second Isaiah, the prophet responsible for Isaiah 40–55, promotes this return. The prophet's poetry conveys both physical and spiritual restoration. It is written exuberantly, brimming with announcements of divine comfort and of Israel's restored standing as God's chosen servant. Unlike earlier prophecies, this poetry isn't characterized by judgment or even by significant ethical instruction. Its rhetoric attempts to finesse a rejoined relationship between Judeans living inside and outside of the land of Judah and to restore confidence in God's favor.

Like other ancient people, Judeans had previously understood that gods inhabited their own respective lands and protected their subjects within those lands. Conventional theology would have taken for granted that Babylon's more powerful gods had defeated Judah's God when Jerusalem fell to the Babylonians. Indeed, Judeans living in exile in Babylon had doubtless become familiar with the magnificent temples and rituals of Marduk and other Babylonian gods who were worshipped in the form of images made of precious metals.

But Second Isaiah develops a new theological claim, one the Western world takes nearly for granted today. The prophet claims that the world isn't populated by multiple deities whose images are housed in temples. Rather, the prophet says, one God made all creation and all people, an invisible God who rejects idols. And this God directs the affairs of all the earth's nations. According to this theology, Israel's God was by no means defeated, but rather allowed Jerusalem's destruction as punishment for Israel's sin (Isa 40:1-2) and now reaches even to Babylon to initiate unfolding events. Israel's God caused the victorious Cyrus from Persia to release captives and to restore devastated habitats, cities, and peoples (Isa 45:1-7).

A new theological claim: The world isn't populated by multiple deities whose images are housed in temples. One God made all creation and all people, an invisible God who rejects idols.

We don't know how many people heeded Second Isaiah's call to return to Jerusalem or whether most people living in Babylon considered this idea attractive. The intensity of Second Isaiah's rhetoric suggests he may have had a challenge in convincing his contemporaries to return to reconstruct Jerusalem. In fact, Jews continued living in Babylon and other lands throughout the centuries. The movement of return began slowly and was conditioned by hardship.

ISAIAH 56–66: PROPHETS OF RENEWAL

Rule by David's descendants wasn't restored in Jerusalem after the Judean exiles returned to it. Rather, under direct Persian rule, the Judean community's leadership in Jerusalem arose from the temple priests and from governors appointed by Persia. Most of Third Isaiah, Isaiah 56–66, deals with life in Jerusalem during Persian times. Several different prophets contributed to this section. Some portions, such as Isaiah 60–62, echo Second Isaiah. Other portions, most vividly Isaiah 58–59 and Isaiah 65–66, echo teaching from First Isaiah. The chapters reflect social struggle and religious innovation. They offer prayers, ethical instruction, and visions for a restored future of peace.

Both Second and Third Isaiah show that there can be differences of opinion among the faithful, even among scriptural writers, especially as new realities challenge settled truths. Second Isaiah challenges previous Israelite self-understandings. Whereas before it had been Judah's own Davidic king who was called God's "anointed," Second Isaiah names the foreign King Cyrus as God's anointed (Isa 45:1). Second Isaiah also envisions the divine promises, previously claimed by Judah's royalty, for the people as a whole. Whereas some roles were previously assigned to select individuals such as Abraham (as God's "friend") and Jeremiah and other prophets (as God's "servants"), Second Isaiah extends the covenant to God's entire people.

Third Isaiah likewise challenges previous assumptions. These chapters continue to promote the social justice already expected in First Isaiah and elsewhere. But these disciples of Isaiah suggest that people once viewed as ineligible for temple service—particularly immigrants and eunuchs—are welcome. They also

There can be differences of opinion among the faithful, even among scriptural writers.

promote the idea that nations and communities will no longer be saved or condemned collectively. Rather, individuals who worship God faithfully, no matter who they are, will be welcomed into the covenant community. But rebels, no matter what their pedigree, will in effect exclude themselves.

A running commentary on "God's servants" begins in Isaiah 41. Throughout much of Second Isaiah, a portrait is drawn of God's servant Israel, who will establish justice, who listens carefully to God's instruction, and who even suffers on others' behalf. In Isaiah 54:17 the plural word *servants* first appears, and in Third Isaiah's final two chapters (Isa 65–66), God's servants are sharply distinguished from those who rebel.

Day 1: Isaiah 40–43
Creation

The first three readings this week come from the prophet of the exile, Second Isaiah, whose speeches in Isaiah 40–55 have been attached to the collection of speeches from the original Isaiah of Jerusalem in Isaiah 1–39. Beginning in Isaiah 40:12, God's role as creator is explored: The one who made everything, with whom none can compare, can and will restore Israel.

Second Isaiah was directed toward a very specific purpose long ago. Yet, as we overhear words addressed to ancient people, we remember with gratitude the prophets who inspired the community's rebuilding. Had this return not taken place, faith would not have developed as it did. There would have been no Judaism, no Bible, no Jewish savior of the Gentiles, and no Christianity.

As the author envisions divine compassion for ancient people, we may find ourselves envisioning a God who creates, re-creates, and rejuvenates, who does new things, who calls the faithful, who loves and comforts the refugee, who encourages the discouraged, and who heals the scarred earth.

Does God always give second chances? What example would you give?

Day 2: Isaiah 49:1–52:12
Comfort

Isaiah 44–48 continues to develop themes found in the reading for Day 1. A corner is turned at Isaiah 49. Here the servant from Isaiah 42 reappears, telling his own story now, echoing themes from throughout the previous poetry. The world's natural elements are again invited to rejoice, celebrating God's comfort for suffering people.

From this point through Isaiah 54, poetry about the servant will be interwoven with poetry concerning Daughter Zion, the personified city of Jerusalem, who speaks up for the first time in Isaiah 49:14. Like Israel the servant, who expressed hopelessness in Isaiah 40:27, here Zion likewise protests that she has been abandoned by God. Like Israel, she receives reassurance. God is portrayed as the city's mother who will never forget her child. The poet envisions Judeans returning in droves to repopulate Jerusalem.

In Isaiah 50, the servant Israel returns, speaking this time of his faithfulness to God even in the face of harassment. His self-description resembles that of the lamenter in Lamentations 3, who recommended faithfulness even in desolation.

The poetry reaches its high point in Isaiah 51–52. After a reminder of Israel's deep historical roots in Abraham and Sarah, God's powerful arm is invoked to act on the people's behalf, as in the exodus from Egypt. Reassurances of God's comfort for suffering Zion are offered repeatedly. The prophet envisions the lookouts, rejoicing as God and an exiled people return to Zion.

Although this poetry addressed a specific moment, the themes of divine comfort and human faithfulness transcend time and give reassurance to believers today of God's extraordinary perseverance with humans throughout history.

Can you think of an example in recent history or even in your community where God's comfort gave refuge to a group of people?

Day 3: Isaiah 52:13–55:13
Restoration

This section begins with a passage referring to a suffering servant, a passage most familiar to Christians in relation to Jesus' crucifixion (Isa 52:13–53:12). It originally referred not to Jesus but to suffering Israel, reassuring the troubled that faithful endurance on behalf of others can itself be redemptive. Early Christians naturally thought of this passage when they examined Jesus' story. It became a sign of hope for people following Jesus' example of patient suffering (see 1 Pet 2:21-25).

The poetry continues to alternate between Israel as God's servant and Daughter Zion. The subject turns abruptly in Isaiah 54 to Jerusalem. Again she is instructed to rejoice in expectation of her "children's" return, and she is reassured by God. Here God takes the role of her formerly angry but now remorseful spouse. As in Noah's covenant, God promises never to destroy again and assures the people that God's covenant of peace will endure (Isa 54:9-10).

The final chapter of Second Isaiah, Isaiah 55, begins with an invitation to enjoy free food and drink, contrasting sharply with realities in a drought-ridden world. The people are invited to seek God, whose forgiveness is generous, whose ways are higher than human ways, and whose covenant with them is everlasting. Rejoicing mountains and hand-clapping trees will welcome Judeans homeward.

Parts of Second Isaiah's poetry may ring familiar to contemporary Christians—not only the description of the servant who bears suffering for others' sake, but also the God whose ways are higher than human ways, who comforts those who mourn, who rescues us from our troubles.

Have you ever suffered in order to relieve suffering for someone else? Or think of a loss that you experienced and reflect on who helped you mourn.

Day 4: Isaiah 56:1-8; 58–61
Justice

The last two readings this week come from prophets in Jerusalem after the exile, whose speeches have been gathered in Isaiah 56–66 and are described collectively as Third Isaiah. First Isaiah (Isa 1–39) preached righteousness and justice in human dealings. Second Isaiah (Isa 40–55) announced that God would comfort and do the right thing on behalf of God's people. Third Isaiah (Isa 56–66) begins with a verse uniting both these themes. Isaiah 56 goes on to announce God's welcome of immigrants and eunuchs. The term "immigrant" here is our English idiom for the Hebrew expression "sons of foreigners," which is a designation for non-Israelites. *Eunuch* is a Greek word for an obscure Hebrew term that some think referred to sexually mutilated men. This claim to include the immigrant and the eunuch in the covenant community, contrary to Deuteronomy 23:1-3, shows how scripture contains more than one point of view about God's Instruction (Torah).

Isaiah 58 resumes the call to social justice, first introduced in Isaiah 1. This chapter promotes care for the needy as crucial to honest piety. In fact, the prophet claims, Jerusalem's physical restoration depends on the strength of its social fabric. The same social ills that plagued the city before its destruction still plague the generations that follow—yet the prophet still calls for justice and continues to hope in God's salvation.

Most of Third Isaiah follows this thread of moral teaching and judgment, underscoring the difficulties of building a faithful city. But in the very center, Isaiah 60–62 envisions a future much more glorious than past or present. This prophet, just as Second Isaiah, assures the people that God's covenant with them will endure (Isa 61:8), no matter what happens in their lives. Thus, in Third Isaiah, judgment and hope intertwine. Inaccessible dreams and unrelenting judgments can each lead to despair. But the two together, tempering each other, can keep us mindful both of frustrations and of hopes that goad us onward.

Do you dream of a world where justice always prevails? Is that possible?

Day 5: Isaiah 63:7–66:24
Presence

This final section of Third Isaiah opens with a cry for help in Isaiah 63:7–64:12. It clearly reflects the time in Jerusalem before the temple was rebuilt there, perhaps even before exiled Judeans had returned home. Petitioners recall God's ancient saving grace before asking that God look down, remember them again, and return to heal the city. In Isaiah 65, the prophet asserts that God is likewise eager for reconciliation. Yet rebellious behavior persists. A distinction is drawn between those who behave as God's servants and those who continue to rebel, who won't enjoy God's bounty.

In Isaiah 65:17-25, a renewed heaven and earth are described, echoing hopes from Isaiah 2:2-4 and Isaiah 11:1-9. An era of earthly prosperity is imagined, when all may live their natural lives in peace.

Isaiah 66 continues visions of prosperous security in Jerusalem, with all but the rebels enjoying worship together. In spite of these glorious visions of renewal, Isaiah's final verse underlies the description of "hell"—actually *Gehenna*—in Mark 9:48. It is so disturbing that, in Jewish traditional readings of Isaiah, verse 23 is repeated afterward, allowing the book's final word to describe all humanity worshipping God, rather than the horror awaiting rebels.

Second and Third Isaiah convey years of Judean experience and thought. They reflect tragedy and resilience, exile and renewal. They show faith being reshaped through suffering. They reflect the perennial struggles between generosity and purity, between self-seeking and self-giving. These prophets don't resolve all questions. But in entertaining these questions, they invite us to rethink and broaden our understanding of God's ways.

Do you have optimism for your community and the wider world you live in? If not, what would restore your hope?

Day 6: Isaiah 43:1-7

Covenant Meditation: Hope comes from God.

In this week's readings, we learned that in a period where "the unspeakable extent of the trauma" experienced by God's people could barely be spoken, the writers of the time ensured that "scripture as we know it was preserved, shaped, and reborn in tragedy and suffering." Since that time, God's people have turned to this poetry of scripture because hope comes from God, and God is always with us. When facing grief and tragedy of our own, we can lose sight of or take for granted God's promise of hope and salvation, but these words from the prophets are forever present to guide us back to God's covenant promises if we will take them to heart. Today we will examine our hearts through the reading practice of *lectio divina*.

Turn to and mark Isaiah 43:1-7. Now take the time you need to become comfortable, calming your breath and releasing into God's hands all the current distractions of the day. It may help to close your eyes until you feel still enough to receive this text. Once you are ready to read, open your Bible to the selected passage and read it aloud slowly for a first reading.

Wait for a minute before reading it a second time. When you are ready, read it slowly again, aloud or silently. This time, listen for a word or phrase from the text that catches your attention. As before, don't try to analyze or judge the word or phrase that you receive. Just note it; write it down or underline it if you would like. For the next two minutes, reflect on this word or phrase. What feelings, images, or memories come to mind from the word or phrase? Note these in your mind or on a piece of paper. Again, just try to receive these and notice them without judgment or analysis.

Read the text for a third time, and attend to any invitation that the reading may extend to you. Does your word or phrase prompt you to some action? Does the whole reading invite you to respond in some fresh way to a circumstance in your life or in God's world? Meditate on this invitation for three or four minutes. Then, in a brief prayer, place into God's hands all that you have received in this practice—your word, phrase, invitation, and response—so that you and God carry these forward together.

Group Meeting Experience

Isaiah 40:12-31 | *God as creator of the world and of Israel*

This passage argues for God's unique power as creator of the cosmos. It may have been composed around the same time as the first creation story in Genesis 1:1–2:4a. Indeed, Second Isaiah shares many ideas with that account. Isaiah 40:12-31 emphasizes God's incomparable greatness and power. It prepares for the argument that God can and will rebuild the nation of Judah.

1. Read Genesis 1:1–2:4a alongside this passage and note similarities and differences between them.
2. Count the rhetorical questions (questions that don't seek to obtain information but to make a point; for example, "Who has measured the waters in the palm of a hand?"). What are they? What are their implied answers?
3. What does the language of measuring and weighing in Isaiah 40:12 convey about God?
4. What purposes might the description of idol-making in Isaiah 40:19-20 serve?
5. In what various ways is God's superior greatness and power conveyed? To whom and what is God compared?
6. What relationship can you see between God's naming of the stars and the claim that God is not ignoring Israel?
7. How is God's incomparable creative power related to the assurance in Isaiah 40:31 that "those who hope in the Lord will renew their strength"?
8. Which images of God in this passage seem familiar to you? Which ones are new? Which linger with you?

SIGNS OF FAITHFUL LOVE

To thrive as hopeful Covenant people, we must keep our eyes on God's purpose, which can be disrupted as much by distraction and complacency as from battlefields and the effects of war.

EPISODE 22

1 and 2 Chronicles, Ezra, Nehemiah

RESTORATION
Rebuilding life together

Bible Readings

Day 1: 1 Chronicles 10:1–11:9; 28–29

Day 2: 2 Chronicles 33–36

Day 3: Ezra 1; 2:68–6:22

Day 4: Ezra 7–10

Day 5: Nehemiah 1–2; 4; 7:73b–8:18

Day 6: Covenant Meditation on 2 Chronicles 15:12-15

Day 7: Group Meeting Experience with 1 Chronicles 29:10-19

Covenant Prayer

For those who feel distant from God

You are a God ready to forgive, merciful and compassionate, very patient, and truly faithful. (Nehemiah 9:17c)

For those who teach children about God's faithful love

The LORD's faithful love is from forever ago to forever from now for those who honor him. And God's righteousness reaches to the grandchildren of those who keep his covenant and remember to keep his commands. (Psalm 103:17-18)

OUR LONGING FOR RELATIONSHIP

After a time of loss, tragedy, or shame is behind us, we're relieved but often frustrated by "the new normal." We've changed, and those around us have changed.

AFTER THE EXILE

The exile officially ended when Cyrus declared that the people from Judah (who were banished to Babylon) could return to their land and "build the house of the Lord" in Jerusalem (Ezra 1:3; 2 Chron 36:23). After the Persians conquered the Babylonian Empire in 539 BCE, the new rulers overturned earlier political policy and allowed all of those who had been deported by the Babylonians to return to their lands. According to Cyrus' edict, the exiles were given a change of residential address, and the people were allowed to return to rebuild the temple and worship together as God's people. In their distinct ways, the books of Chronicles, Ezra, and Nehemiah each configure the renewal of a community placing the worship of God in Jerusalem at the center of its life.

EZRA

The book of Ezra emphasizes this theme in its depiction of several waves of returnees who determine to worship God in their reconstructed temple. The various returns, led by Sheshbazzar in Ezra 1 and by Ezra in Ezra 6–7, seem almost like pilgrimages with their emphases on generous offerings, worship equipment, and God's guidance. These narratives repeat that the people aren't simply returning to the land. Their true destination is Jerusalem itself and the restoration of God's temple there (Ezra 1:3; 6:8; 7:7-8, 13; 8:31-32). Fittingly, upon their arrival, the groups present their offerings in the holy area where their temple once stood (Ezra 2:68-69; 8:33-35).

The first group of returnees meant to restore the temple and reestablish worship in Jerusalem. Ezra's initial chapters tell of the attempts to rebuild first the altar, then the foundation of the temple, and finally the temple itself. Again and again, however, detractors frustrate their efforts, including the neighboring peoples and Tattenai, governor of the province Beyond the River. Significantly, the returnees themselves turn away offers of help. One group, for example, asks to join in the construction because "we worship your God as you do, and we've been sacrificing to him ever since the days of Assyria's King Esarhaddon" (Ezra 4:2). These advances are rejected because the returnees consider this group as enemies rather than religious allies (Ezra 4:1).

Ezra's initial chapters tell of the attempts to rebuild first the altar, then the foundation of the temple, and finally the temple itself.

The narrative in Ezra evokes uneasy tension as it struggles to redefine community by setting rules for inclusion in the restored community and teaching how communal worship should be practiced in Jerusalem. In Ezra 6:21, participation in the Passover Festival is open to all who joined the community, yet the book concludes with the call to expel the foreign women who married into the community (Ezra 9–10). Clearly the stakes are high, as the returnees are understandably conservative in their decisions and cautious about provoking the divine ire and bringing about another exile. Restoration in Ezra thus means more than return to the land and rebuilding the temple. It involves the serious task of setting out the proper limits for the worshipping community.

NEHEMIAH

In the book of Nehemiah, these limits take on a physical dimension when Governor Nehemiah sets out to repair Jerusalem's protective walls. When he hears a report that the walls were broken down and that the gates had burned, Nehemiah sets out for Jerusalem (Neh 1:3; 2:5). Upon his arrival, he leads the community to repair the edifice section by section. As in the book of Ezra, the people face opposition and setbacks as they build, but they ultimately triumph. With the wall built, they are able to protect the restored community, whose members are trying to observe the covenant, follow God's Instruction, and worship according to divine teaching.

As they tell the story about the return to the land, the books of Ezra and Nehemiah incorporate official documents such as imperial edicts (Ezra 1:2-4), letters to the king (Ezra 5:6-17), and genealogical records (Ezra 2). The inclusion of these documents indicates that written records now have authority for the returning Israelite exiles. Given this special appreciation of official documents, some of the returnees themselves wrote down a version of their nation's earliest history. These documents articulate their ancient past and their distinct view of what true restoration might look like in the present. The author of this history used one of his people's own documents, which we call the Deuteronomistic History (see Episode 8), as the basis for this new version of Israelite history. And thus we have Chronicles, whose author, the Chronicler, tells the story of Israel from the time of Adam through the end of the exile.

1 AND 2 CHRONICLES

Although the books of Chronicles retell events *before* the time of Ezra and Nehemiah, they appear to have actually been written *later* in the period after the exile. The narratives in Chronicles reflect some of the same values as Ezra and Nehemiah, but they also take a unique view on some key issues. One of these distinctive views relates to the definition of *community*. The destruction of Jerusalem and the exile of its people began the diaspora, the dispersion of the Jews outside of Israel, not just to Babylon but to other countries throughout the Middle East. The Chronicler takes this larger context seriously and expands the limits of community beyond those assumed in Ezra and Nehemiah. Whereas the southern tribes of Benjamin and Judah are predominant in the earlier books, the Chronicler includes the northern tribes, united in worship with the southern tribes, as the ideal manifestation of the nation. The Chronicler also takes a much different attitude toward intermarriage. Instead of seeing all marriage outside the tribe as a threat that must be strictly opposed, the Chronicler includes notices of such intermarriage without censure (1 Chron 2:3; 3:2, and so on). Like the author of the book of Ruth, the Chronicler considers intermarriage as a way to grow and strengthen the people of Israel.

> **Optional:** *An additional video on exile and the return to worship in Jerusalem is available for download from* **CovenantBibleStudy.com**.

All of these books are united by the central place they give to Jerusalem in the people's lives and worship. In Chronicles, kings who support the temple are rewarded by God, and those who harm it or encourage worship elsewhere are punished. Indeed, there is a sense that Jerusalem's centrality is meant to become a way of life. This is underscored when 1 and 2 Chronicles are read in the context of the Jewish Bible, where they appear as the final books in the canon, making Cyrus' edict to rebuild the temple the final words of the Hebrew scriptures. In this literary setting, the end of Chronicles urges the faithful throughout the ages to claim their true identity, working to restore God's worship in Jerusalem: "Whoever among you belong to God's people, let them go up, and may the Lord their God be with them!" (2 Chron 36:23).

Day 1: 1 Chronicles 10:1–11:9; 28–29
The temple at the center of the community

The Chronicler abbreviates Saul's reign from twenty-three chapters (1 Sam 9–31) to a single chapter (1 Chron 10). Then he moves on to a more central interest: David and his preparations to build the temple. The account of David's rule extends for nineteen long chapters and is marked by a focused attention on Jerusalem and the temple. The importance of Jerusalem is demonstrated immediately by David's capture of the city in his first act as king (1 Chron 11). And when David's death looms in 1 Chronicles 28–29, his final words emphasize his extensive preparations for the temple that his son Solomon will build, the temple that will house the record of God's covenant with Israel (1 Chron 28:2). Thus the author emphasizes that David's rule extends far beyond the account of his reign: Future worship in the temple will be permanently marked by David's pioneering efforts, and future kings will be measured against his devotion to God's house in Jerusalem.

How important is it to have holy space, a place where people worship?

Day 2: 2 Chronicles 33–36
Return and restoration

Just as the Chronicler significantly revised the Deuteronomistic Historian's account of Saul, so the Chronicler takes the story of Manasseh from 2 Kings and reshapes it according to his specific emphases. In the book of Kings, Manasseh is Judah's worst ruler, committing serious sins regarding temple worship, leading the nation to do the same, and dying without changing his ways (2 Kgs 21). These deeds were so terrible that the Deuteronomistic Historian found in them the grounds for the exile of the nation years later (2 Kgs 24:3-4). Chronicles nuances this presentation in 2 Chronicles 33. To be sure, Manasseh commits many sins. But while being punished in exile, he seeks and receives God's forgiveness. After he is restored to the land, he spends the rest of his reign removing the foreign altars.

This version of Manasseh's reign stresses the immediacy of retribution, which is the same theology at the heart of the Deuteronomistic History: The king is punished for his sins, and the generation who went into exile are themselves to blame, rather than a long-dead king (2 Chron 36:6, 14-15). But the Chronicler's account also stresses the possibility of restoration: If even Manasseh can be forgiven and returned to the land, then anyone can certainly expect that they will be forgiven if they return to God. The Chronicler also highlights the significance of proper worship in Jerusalem. Second Chronicles ends, in fact, with Cyrus' edict directing the people of Judah and Jerusalem to reconstruct the temple at the center of their restored community.

When disasters occur in our country, is that a sign of God's punishment?

Day 3: Ezra 1; 2:68–6:22
Rebuilding

In response to Cyrus' edict allowing the Jews to return to Jerusalem around 539 BCE, the people set out under the leadership of Sheshbazzar (Ezra 1). He is succeeded by Jeshua (a priest) and Zerubbabel (an heir of David), who lead the people in rebuilding the altar (Ezra 3:1-6) and in laying the temple's foundation (Ezra 3:8-13). Local opposition to their work is described in Ezra 4:1-5, 24. As Zerubbabel and the community renew their attempt to rebuild the temple in Ezra 5, a report is sent by opposing forces to Darius, questioning the people's authority to undertake the reconstruction. After Darius does his own research of earlier edicts in Ezra 6, he allows the building to continue, and the people complete the temple around 520 BCE.

These chapters maintain a clear emphasis on the people's determination to rebuild the temple in Jerusalem as the focus of their new community and on the strength of the outside forces opposing this. With such a presentation, the author can highlight the temple's significance for the restored community while explaining the nearly forty-year delay in its completion.

When people are displaced by war, disaster, and famine, why are survivors so determined to rebuild?

Day 4: Ezra 7–10
Ezra continues the restoration.

About sixty years after the temple was completed, Ezra, a scribe with expert knowledge of the covenant, "the Instruction from Moses" (Ezra 7:6), obtained permission from King Artaxerxes to return with another group of Jews to Jerusalem to continue the efforts at restoration. Before setting out, Ezra received instructions from King Artaxerxes to "investigate Judah and Jerusalem according to the Instruction from your God, which is in your hand" (that is, a written record of the covenant), and to convey the empire's offering to the temple (Ezra 7:14-19). The very large donation of silver, gold, and temple equipment showcases the strong support of the Persian establishment for the temple (Ezra 8:26-27). Given the amount of opposition that the community faced, such support from the highest authorities must have been very welcome. The additional offerings from those who remained in Babylon highlight the temple's far-flung influence (Ezra 8:25).

Ezra's immediate task is to respond to the practice of intermarriage and to the larger issue of the definition and limits of the covenant community. Upon arrival, Ezra is immediately told that some have intermarried with the "peoples of the neighboring lands" (Ezra 9:1-2). Ezra's prayer judges the welfare of the people based entirely on whether they have observed the prohibition of intermarriage with the neighboring peoples. The focus on this particular covenantal responsibility alone, and the call for the expulsion of the foreign women, is disturbing. It points to the great threat that the small and vulnerable community believed they faced and to their struggle to preserve their community in the face of serious threats to its survival. Although the community acted quickly and in solidarity here, there are indications that not all members of the community supported the expulsion. Curiously, the book of Ezra never actually explicitly reports that the women were sent away. Intermarriage continues to be practiced in the time of Nehemiah (Neh 13:23), and other contemporaneous texts, such as Chronicles and Ruth, emphasize the beneficial effects that marriages with foreigners can have upon the nation. It appears that a lively debate continued in the community after the exile about how exclusive or inclusive their community should be.

Why do some groups oppose intermarriage? In addition to marriage across racial groups, what other kinds of intermarriage are often opposed by some members of a group?

Day 5: Nehemiah 1–2; 4; 7:73b–8:18
Nehemiah rebuilds walls; Ezra renews the covenant.

When he hears that the walls of Jerusalem were broken down, Nehemiah sets out to lead the community in making repairs (Neh 1–2; 4). As in the book of Ezra, the people face many difficulties in their efforts to rebuild Jerusalem, but they finally succeed. And when they do, they mark their success by joining together to renew the covenant under Ezra's leadership (Neh 7:73b–8:18). Ezra reads from the scroll that contained the covenant and God's Instruction, the Levites interpret Ezra's words to the people, and the people commit themselves to keeping the covenant (Neh 8:1-8; 10:28-29). One of their first acts is to reinstate the religious calendar of ancient Israel. The "seventh month" is the month of Tishrei (our September–October). During this month, the people gather the harvest and celebrate several religious festivals. The booths they construct commemorate the small huts of branches they made in order to stay in the fields during the harvest.

We know from other biblical books that the first day of Tishrei later became known as the New Year Festival, celebrated by the people resting from their labor, joining together, and offering sacrifices (Lev 23:33-43; Num 29:1). This feast was followed by the Day of Reconciliation (or Atonement) on the tenth day of the month, then the weeklong Festival of Booths, which began on the fifteenth day. According to Deuteronomy 31:10-13, contained in the Instruction scroll Ezra read, Moses commanded that every seventh year the Instruction be read to the people gathered for the Festival of Booths. It is probably this instruction that gave rise to the people's request that Ezra read them the teachings from God.

As they gather in the city made secure by the repaired walls, the people celebrate their ancient festivals. In so doing, the community joins with their ancestors, who marked their allegiance to God and to each other by implementing the teachings from Moses.

What festivals do you celebrate in your congregation or home, and how is scripture used in those celebrations? Which one is your favorite festival?

Day 6: 2 Chronicles 15:12-15
Covenant Meditation: Don't abandon each other!

The texts we studied this week from 1 and 2 Chronicles, Ezra, and Nehemiah are rich with details about significant individuals and events in the story of God's covenant people. As we wade into the depths and intricacies of the relationships and transitions revealed in these sacred texts, our inclination is often to retain in memory as much detail as possible to better understand what comes next in the scriptures. This is one of the many lifelong benefits of a comprehensive Bible study. We come to know more of scripture.

But as much as this week's readings instruct and inform our minds and memories, they also offer a way for God to form our hearts as people of faith. Through these readings, we also come to be more known by God. The spiritual reading practice of *lectio divina* will again serve to guide us.

First, go to a space in which you can be fully present to this reading with as few distractions as possible. Locate 2 Chronicles 15:12-15 and mark its place so that you can easily return there. Now take a few moments of quiet time to prepare your heart and life to receive this text freshly. If it helps to close your eyes and focus on your breathing, do so.

When ready, slowly read the whole text (aloud or silently). Then read it a second time, noticing the word or phrase that catches your attention or draws your energy, whether for a positive or a negative reaction. After completing the reading, return to that word or phrase and silently or quietly, perhaps with eyes closed, repeat it slowly several times.

Now read the passage a third time, with your word or phrase in mind. This time, let your thoughts engage the word or phrase. What feelings come to mind as you do so? What reactions do you have? What does your word or phrase bring to mind or spark in your imagination as you think about the whole reading? Take as much time as you need for this and for any questions that form for you. Write these down if you would like. When your thoughts begin to feel repetitive or complete, move on.

Read the passage one last time, and then offer to God all that you have thought about and wondered during this practice of sacred reading. Give God thanks for allowing the word to intersect your life today. Go in peace.

Group Meeting Experience

1 Chronicles 29:10-19 | *David's prayer*

This passage contains the Chronicler's version of David's final prayer—set before the first temple was built, but written after the exile. Knowing that the prayer was read after the exile, we will pay attention to how new concerns shape the covenant relationship between God and the people. By keeping the period of return and restoration in mind, try to answer the following questions:

1. What kind of God does David portray in his prayer? How is God's power manifested?

2. Where is God portrayed as just? Where is God portrayed as free?

3. How are human beings portrayed in this prayer? What is the role of the community?

4. Where do you see the prayer looking ahead toward the exile? Where does the author locate hope?

5. What does true restoration look like in this prayer?

6. What is the function of the temple in Jerusalem and within the restored community?

SIGNS OF FAITHFUL LOVE

After a time of loss or suffering, Covenant people are restored to life and to our true selves when we worship God as the center of our lives.

EPISODE 23

Apocalyptic: Daniel

Hope
Trusting God in times of crisis

Bible Readings

Day 1: Daniel 1–2

Day 2: Daniel 3–4

Day 3: Daniel 6

Day 4: Daniel 7

Day 5: Daniel 9

Day 6: Covenant Meditation on Daniel 9:4-19

Day 7: Group Meeting Experience with Daniel 11:27-35

Covenant Prayer

For those who are harassed or imprisoned for belief in God

Turn to me, God, and have mercy on me because I'm alone and suffering. . . . Look at how many enemies I have and how violently they hate me! Please protect my life! (Psalm 25:16, 19-20a)

For liberators and peacemakers who offer hope where there is no hope

Hope in the Lord! Be strong! Let your heart take courage! Hope in the Lord! (Psalm 27:14)

> **OUR LONGING FOR RELATIONSHIP**
>
> We remain firm in faith, with confidence, during times when our covenant way of life is challenged or when our personal circumstances make us feel anxious, frustrated, and insecure.

APOCALYPTIC LITERATURE

The word *apocalyptic* describes a specific form of religious literature common in Jewish and Christian communities from the third century BCE through the fourth and fifth centuries CE. Although dozens of apocalyptic writings have survived from this period, only two examples are contained in the Christian Bible, namely, the books of Daniel and Revelation. Other parts of the Bible, however, are influenced by apocalyptic thought, including Isaiah 24–27, Zechariah 1–6, 12–14, and notably also the preaching of Jesus (Matt 25; Mark 13:14-36).

The apocalyptic literature in the books of Daniel and Revelation comes from communities living under the duress of foreign colonial powers, whose policies restrict their religious freedoms and even harass them for living out their covenant obligations. These books advocate faithfulness to God's covenant and resistance to the political policies that prohibit observing it. They also express fervent hope for the end of imperial control and the imminent establishment of God's kingdom. Their visions of the end of the empire oppressing them are cloaked in symbolic images that are strange and bizarre, but intended to protect the authors from the consequences of leveling such a direct critique against the ruling authorities.

These strange, symbolic visions of the end of imperial oppression in Daniel and Revelation are often misunderstood by readers today as aimed at some distant future, a future we can figure out if we try to decode these images by connecting them with nations today. In fact, the symbolic images of Daniel and Revelation were directed to the empires of the authors' own times. The divine intervention they expected was imminent, and they hoped it would radically change their own circumstances. What we can learn from these books is not a political map of our own century, but how covenant communities living in very difficult times were able to persevere and not give up hope for a better future.

DANIEL

The presence of two very different literary forms makes the book of Daniel among the most unusual books in the Old Testament. The first half of the book, Daniel 1–6, contains a series of hero stories or resistance stories in which Daniel and his friends provide models of covenant faithfulness and successful resistance to oppressive

The symbolic images of Daniel and Revelation were directed to the empires of the authors' own times.

imperial policies, even at great risk to themselves. The second half of the book, Daniel 7–12, contains three apocalyptic visions predicting the end of oppressive and ruthless human empires and the establishment of God's kingdom on earth.

On top of its two distinct literary forms, the book of Daniel has come to us in two different languages. But the language changes don't coincide with the literary changes. Daniel 1:1–2:4*a* and Daniel 8–12 are written in Hebrew, while Daniel 2:4*b* through Daniel 7 is written in Aramaic, a language closely related to Hebrew that was used for international communication at the time of Daniel, and which eventually replaced Hebrew as the common language of Palestine under Roman rule. The Apocrypha, a collection of books included in Roman Catholic, Greek, and Slavonic Bibles but not found in the Protestant Bible, contains additional material about Daniel: the stories of Susanna and of Bel and the Snake, and the Hymn of the Three Young Men. Our present book of Daniel therefore contains a selection of the "Daniel stories" that were in circulation among Jewish communities in the second century BCE.

The setting for the stories and visions in the book of Daniel is the Babylonian exile (Dan 1:1-2). Daniel is pictured as a hero resisting the Babylonian policies that threatened his covenant loyalties. But evidence in the book indicates that while these stories are set during the Babylonian exile, they were actually written for a later community during its own crisis over its life of faith. The author's memory of the Babylonian period is inexact. Neither the books of 1 and 2 Kings nor Babylonian annals record Nebuchadnezzar's attack on Jerusalem in Jehoiakim's third year (Dan 1:1). Belshazzar wasn't Nebuchadnezzar's son (Dan 5:2), and Babylon fell to Persia's King Cyrus, not to Darius the Mede (Dan 5:30-31), a figure not mentioned in the Bible or other ancient Near Eastern texts. By contrast, Daniel's author knows the history of the later Hellenistic (Greek) period very well. In Daniel 11 he recounts in detail the rise of Alexander the Great (Dan 11:3) and of the Ptolemaic kings of Egypt (Dan 11:5-8) and the Seleucid kings of Syria (Dan 11:9-20) that followed him, focusing in particular on the Seleucid king Antiochus IV (175–164 BCE; Dan 11:21-45), who was responsible for a fierce repression of the Jewish community in and around Jerusalem. This is the crisis during which Daniel was written and for which it was intended. Thus Daniel's experiences and visions of an earlier time were told by a member of the second-century Jewish community to inspire resistance and hope during their own period of oppression. Of course, the truths learned in any such crisis have a broader, universal value.

Court stories of Daniel 1–6: The intention of the stories in Daniel 1–6 is debated. If the stories are read as instructions to exiles for successful living while in exile (sometimes called the diaspora) outside of Judah and Jerusalem, then they are considered more hopeful. In fact, the stories of Daniel and his friends in the courts of kings in Daniel 1–6 seem friendlier to an empire than the visions of Daniel 7–12, which predict their violent demise. If, on the other hand, one notes the threats of horrific forms of punishment in these stories and the context of danger for the exiles practicing their covenant faith, then the stories take on a much darker tone, and they could be seen as encouraging resistance in the diaspora communities experiencing serious harassment and punishment. Recent readings of the Daniel stories are more attuned to the social and political resistance by minorities in circumstances of subordination. These readings are inspiring to the communities that suffered under the powerful colonial empires of the nineteenth and twentieth centuries CE.

> **Optional:** *An additional video on how contemporary communities identify with stories about Daniel is available for download from* **CovenantBibleStudy.com**.

Apocalyptic visions of Daniel 7–12: The symbolic visions in Daniel 7–12 are deeply concerned about making sense of the violent events of the second century during the reign of Antiochus IV (175–164 BCE). The visions express hope for a restoration of the Jewish people experiencing severe harassment (Dan 12:11-13). There are three distinct visions: Daniel 7, Daniel 8, and an extended vision in Daniel 10–12. The visions are interrupted in Daniel 9 by a prayer in which Daniel asks for God's help in the midst of a confession of sin that reviews the mistakes of Israel's past.

The Hellenistic ruler in Mesopotamia and Palestine, Antiochus IV, tried to expand his rule into Egypt but was forced to stop by Rome. In Jerusalem there was open revolt, initiated by a group within the Jewish community known as the Maccabees who thought Antiochus was in a weakened position. Antiochus IV's response was violent. Many Jews were killed or sold into slavery, and the Jerusalem temple was violated. Furthermore, the apocryphal book of 1 Maccabees indicates that there were Jews on many sides of this conflict and that they were divided into factions. The author of Daniel may well have been a member of one of these groups that self-identified as the "Maskilim," the "teachers" (or "wise ones"), who appear to be addressed in a "call to action" in Daniel 11:33-35. Their resistance was religious rather than military—and their visions were expressions of their deepest hopes for God's intervention in the conflicts.

Day 1: Daniel 1–2
The emperor's dream

Daniel 1 identifies Daniel and his three friends as members of Jerusalem's ruling class whom King Nebuchadnezzar deported to Babylon after attacking Jerusalem, and it explains how these young Judean exiles became important figures in the royal court of Babylon. This story describes Daniel and his friends' first act of civil disobedience (see Day 3): They refused to obey laws they believed would compromise their covenant obligations.

Daniel 2 describes their second great crisis. The conqueror of Jerusalem is having trouble sleeping. It isn't, apparently, out of regret for the thousands he had killed by his imperial conquests—rather, it is the result of a terrifying dream. He knows what he saw, but he doesn't know what it means. Dreams were believed to have power—even power over an emperor—and we know from ancient sources that they believed the way to break the power of a mysterious and threatening dream was to have it interpreted. Daniel, by God's inspiration, is able to advise the conqueror. And his advice? Effectively, it is to tell the king that his mighty kingdom won't be around much longer!

Each part of the great statue in this dream represents an ancient kingdom referred to elsewhere in the book of Daniel: Babylon's King Nebuchadnezzar is the head of gold (Dan 2:38), Darius the Mede is the chest of silver (Dan 5:30-31), Persia's King Cyrus is the torso of bronze (Dan 6:28), Greece's Alexander the Great is represented by the legs of iron (Dan 8:20-21), and the Ptolemies and Seleucids who followed Alexander and ruled in the author's own day are the feet of iron and clay (Dan 11). The dream predicts the demise of them all, including the Seleucids who were brutally harassing the Jews at the time that the book of Daniel was written. Daniel's message to the tyrant is our message to all conquerors, ancient and modern: Your kingdom of death can only be short-lived. God's reign of life and justice approaches!

How do you define tyrant? Who are the tyrants today?

Day 2: Daniel 3–4
The emperor's madness

Daniel 3–4 follows the same sequence as the stories in Daniel 1–2: An account of civil disobedience is followed by the king's dream symbolizing God's punishment of the empire. In Daniel 3, Daniel's three friends refuse to bow before the image of the king and his power, and they are thrown into the furnace, only to be miraculously protected by God. As in Daniel 1, they refuse to compromise their covenant obligations even when threatened by death.

> **Optional:** *An additional video retelling the story of Shadrach, Meshach, and Abednego is available for download from* **CovenantBibleStudy.com**.

The two stories in Daniel 4 must be read as interlaced. The tree hovers over the animals (the Babylonian Empire hovering over the conquered peoples) until God "frees" the animals by chopping down the tree. The story of Nebuchadnezzar's madness (he eats grass like a cow) makes sense in the context of the other story. In a classic reversal of fortune, Nebuchadnezzar must experience what it's like to be an "animal," that is, a conquered person. The resistant "humor" of oppressed peoples is often contained in such stories that change circumstances for the better. Daniel's author views the empire and its power ambiguously. It can feed and protect its people (Dan 4:10-12), but it can also become proud and abuse them (Dan 4:26-27).

What covenant obligation(s) would you refuse to compromise?

Gandhi has said that in Daniel 6 we see the greatest "passive resister" in history.

Day 3: Daniel 6
Civil disobedience

Generations of readers of Daniel have read the famous "Lion's Den" story as a story about the importance of standing firm for one's faith and about the importance of prayer. These convictions are important, but there is more to this story. When he came out of one of his first imprisonments in South Africa, Gandhi announced that in Daniel 6 we see the greatest "passive resister" (his term for nonviolent action) in history. Gandhi calls our attention to Daniel 6:10 and suggests that Daniel intentionally broke an unjust law. In fact, we can read this passage actively—that Daniel *himself* threw open the windows in order to make his prayers public! When is it important, in the words of Peter, to obey God rather than humans (Acts 5:29)?

In our culture, what are the options for disobeying the will of the majority? Are any of your faith or covenant practices considered illegal?

Day 4: Daniel 7
Fifth monarchy

The first vision of the second half of the book of Daniel picks up the "series of four" theme of Daniel 2, where four kingdoms—Babylon, Media, Persia, and Greece—follow one after the other in world history. Here, alluding to a primordial "battle" with beings from the sea, four beasts (or kingdoms), arise. They are composite creatures, mixing ferocious beasts. (The image of the fourth beast may be drawn from battle elephants; see also Dan 7:19.) The fact that they are mixed adds to the horror—especially in a context where Jews were being pressured to conform and give up their distinctive religious traditions (and thus become "mixed")! The final extraordinary beast is Antiochus IV, who attacks the Jewish community and outlaws its covenant obligations (Dan 7:25).

Optional: *An additional video on the "one like a human being" (or "Son of Man") and Jesus is available for download from* **CovenantBibleStudy.com**.

The beasts as world kingdoms leave little doubt about the political sympathies of the visionary. When God, "the ancient one" (Dan 7:9), arrives for judgment, power and authority are given over to the "one like a human being" (Dan 7:13), who descends from the clouds (as opposed to the beasts who arise from the sea). This descending figure likely represents Michael, the angelic protector of Israel and God's warrior—symbolizing God's kingdom and its ultimate victory. Christians later saw in this human figure an image of Jesus inaugurating God's kingdom. For early Christians to see Jesus in this role would have been courageous, contrasting Jesus against the violence and depravity of worldly kingdoms, in particular the Roman Empire under which they lived.

As you look at the state of the world, with one war after another between nations and empires, what role do you think Jesus plays now and in the future?

Day 5: Daniel 9
Daniel's prayer

Daniel 9 is an interesting interlude in a series of bizarre visions, and it is an example of prayer that became standard in Jewish communities after the exile. It is known as the "Penitential Prayer" (compare Ezra 9 and Neh 9). At the heart of this type of prayer was a confession that the events of the exile—and the continued life of diaspora outside Judah and occupation within Judah—was "our fault" because their ancestors had listened to the kings rather than the prophets and had disobeyed the covenant commandments (presumably alluding to the warnings in Deut 28 to cast them out of the land). This type of prayer appears in books separated by hundreds of years (including the very late apocryphal book of Baruch), and thus it was practiced for a long time. The prayer is not only a summary of history, but also a warning to observe covenant obligations and not to take chances with ignoring God's instructions in the future! These prayers remind us of the proper way forward by not repeating the mistakes of the past.

Should our prayers confess historical mistakes by a whole group of people more often?

Day 6: Daniel 9:4-19
Covenant Meditation: Trusting the covenant

Our devotional practice today will return us to one of the most essential and life-giving means by which to engage God's word. We will pray the scripture, or, more precisely, we will invite the scripture to become a prayer in us. With our week's theme of "Hope," especially when confronted by destructive political or institutional powers, prayer that arises from God's word is prayer grounded in God's hope.

Find a place in which you can be as undisturbed and quiet as possible for this reading time. Turn to Daniel 9:4-19, and mark this reading so that you can easily find it after a minute or two of silent prayer. In this silent prayer time, ask God to help you to be open to this reading in new ways and to remove any distractions from your thoughts that might interfere with your encounter and response to this text. After your silent prayer, slowly read Daniel 9:4-19, attending to each word and phrase.

When you have finished the reading, return to the text and choose one phrase or verse from the prayer that catches your attention for any reason. As best you can, resist analyzing your selection, but try instead to receive the phrase as a prayer for you. Use the phrase or verse to create your own one-sentence prayer. This selection can be exactly as it is translated in your reading, or you may want to develop your own short prayer. For example, if Daniel 9:9 is what catches your attention, your prayer might be: "Thank you, God, for your compassion and deep forgiveness." Take a few minutes to find and create your prayer out of this scripture. Write it down, and then, in silence or aloud, repeat your prayer a few times now and, if possible, off and on throughout the day. This is a prayer for your life arising from your encounter with God's word. Through this practice, we are trusting God's covenant of hope through our prayers.

Group Meeting Experience

Daniel 11:27-35 | What about apocalyptic visions?

While many Christians have read the apocalyptic books of Daniel and Revelation as political maps of the contemporary world and as codes to unlock the secrets of the end time, these books actually describe attempts by ancient covenant communities to live faithfully under government regimes that forced them to compromise their values and loyalty to their faith.

1. How does this text about the policies and exploits of the Seleucid king Antiochus IV describe the exercise of political power? Compare this portrait of him with the one you read in Daniel 7 (Day 4).

2. How does the portrait of political power in these visions compare or contrast with the way royal power is exercised in the stories you read in Daniel 1–6 (Days 1–3)? Do the portraits of power in Daniel teach us anything about the exercise of power in today's world? In what ways do governments today ask occupied peoples or their own citizens to compromise their religious values?

3. The "people's teachers" in this text (Dan 11:33, 35) may represent a group of faithful Jews of which the author of Daniel was a member. How do they appear to respond to political oppression?

4. Compare the "teachers'" response to political repression with the response of Daniel and his friends in the stories of Daniel 1–6. How does the author of Daniel view civil disobedience? What are the merits of this approach over the armed resistance of the Maccabees (described in the Old Testament Apocrypha books of 1 and 2 Maccabees)? How do we respond to political power today that we believe compromises our religious values?

5. The visions of Daniel about the end of an empire and its repressive policies are meant to provide hope for a covenant community in distress. How do visions about the just rule of God provide power to endure suffering and to remain faithful to God's covenant?

SIGNS OF FAITHFUL LOVE

We show loyal love and compassion to anyone who is harassed or oppressed, just as we remain faithful in our relationship with God when our commitments are unpopular or inconvenient.

EPISODE 24

Revelation

NEW CREATION
Trusting God, who makes all things new

Bible Readings

Day 1: Revelation 1–3
Day 2: Revelation 4:1–8:1
Day 3: Revelation 12–14
Day 4: Revelation 15–17
Day 5: Revelation 19–22
Day 6: Covenant Meditation on Revelation 7:9-17
Day 7: Group Meeting Experience: Our covenant

Covenant Prayer

For all who are endangered and harassed because of their faith

Because you kept my command to endure, I will keep you safe through the time of testing that is about to come. (Revelation 3:10)

For all who teach nonviolence and live for peace in the world

You have heard that it was said, You must love your neighbor and hate your enemy. But I say to you, love your enemies and pray for those who harass you so that you will be acting as children of your Father who is in heaven. (Matthew 5:43-45)

OUR LONGING FOR RELATIONSHIP

The world seems full of enemies and hostility. Evil acts in our communities make us fearful and challenge our courage to endure as Christ's followers.

BOOK OF REVELATION

The book of Revelation can be a very confusing book. So it's not surprising that many readers have misunderstood its imagery and warnings, which can result in bizarre predictions as well as disastrous consequences for gullible believers who followed a false leader. We proceed then with a sense of humility and awe as we examine an imaginative call to be faithful witnesses. We are urged through this book to inhabit a renewed heaven and earth and to become citizens of the New Jerusalem (Rev 21:1-2).

Revelation is written by a seer named John (Rev 1:1). For a variety of reasons, it's unlikely that this is the same author who wrote John's Gospel or 1, 2, and 3 John. The author identifies himself as a prophet. He assumes pastoral authority over churches in seven particular cities, and he is the recipient of a mystical vision of Jesus. Revelation was written during the reign of either Emperor Nero (54–68 CE) or Domitian (81–96 CE). When Revelation was written, there was little historical evidence that the entire Roman Empire was engaged in the systematic harassment and killing of early Christians. However, a regional repression probably did occur.

The residents of Roman Asia viewed their rulers as worthy recipients of religious honors. The rulers assumed or were granted the status of divine or semi-divine beings. This kind of emperor worship caused regional and local officials, as well as neighbors, to put pressure on Christians to conform to intolerable religious customs. Additionally, all seven cities in Revelation 2–3 were official sites recognized for emperor worship between 30 BCE and 130 CE. This tradition of granting allegiance to the emperor, to Caesar, would have seemed normal to most people. Anyone who refused to take part would have been seen as rebellious. Christian monotheism prohibited Christians from easily participating in worship of the ruler, making Christians open to ridicule and harassment.

In 1 Corinthians, the apostle Paul gives advice to Christians about whether it is acceptable to eat meat that was, before it was purchased, offered to idols. This raises issues of accommodation, especially when Christians need a meal. Compare Paul's advice about dealing with religious customs in 1 Corinthians 8–10 to John's dilemma over accepting the authority of local leaders who obey the emperor.

Apocalypse: The book of Revelation has actually become the name of an entire type of literature. The first word of the book is *apokalupsis*, a revelation or disclosure of hidden heavenly truths. An apocalypse often includes: (1) a vision of a new world order; (2) a heavenly mediator; (3) a human seer of high repute; (4) writing offered under the name or byline of a hero from the past (meaning that the author is "pseudonymous"); (5) a reimagination of traditions; (6) "prophecy-after-the-fact"; (7) history as predetermined and human society as dualistic; (8) holy numbers to convey meaning; and (9) origins in a marginalized or disenfranchised group. Other apocalyptic writings from this era include Daniel 7–12 in the Old Testament (see Episode 23) and several books from the Old Testament Apocrypha, including 2 Esdras (also called 4 Ezra), 2 Baruch, and 1 Enoch.

Revelation varies from the pattern because it wasn't written under a pseudonym. The writer describes it as a prophecy (not an apocalypse), and it has the features of a letter, which aren't found in other apocalypses. So Revelation is a mix of three genres: apocalypse, letter, and prophecy.

Revelation is meant to be heard. It's a very noisy book. Thus many hymns and poems are based on it. It's also visually powerful. Revelation has inspired the world's most admired visual artists (and some of that art scrolls across the Covenant table for this video episode). Much of the imagery is bizarre and fantastic, but it's meant to excite all the senses and stoke the imagination. Sometimes imagination is the gift God expects us to rely upon most heavily when we find ourselves in territory that is unsafe and uncomfortable.

Purpose: The purpose of the book of Revelation is to lead God's people on a final spiritual exodus to the New Jerusalem. Along the way, Christians must remain firm in their practices and fight evil with a faithful witness. Christians must never lose hope, no matter how bleak the trouble and social circumstances.

Christians never give up because God Almighty is the creator and Lord of the universe. God shares divine authority with Christ (Rev 2:28). God and Christ control history (Rev 1:4, 8, 17). Both are worshipped (Rev 5:13). Both protect the saints (Rev 7:14-17). Both reign in the New Jerusalem (Rev 21:22-27). Both are trustworthy and true (Rev 19:11; 21:5). God Almighty will dwell with the saints who reach the New Jerusalem (Rev 21).

Revelation offers a distinctive understanding of the Messiah, who is defined by the crucifixion. Christ is the slain Lamb. In Revelation 5, John weeps when no one is found worthy to open the scroll. Unless someone opens the scroll, God's plan can't come to fruition. An angel tells John that the Lion of the tribe of Judah is worthy to

The purpose of the book of Revelation is to lead God's people on a final spiritual exodus to the New Jerusalem.

open the scroll. The "Lion of Judah" is a metaphor for the Davidic messiah. However, when John turns he sees not a lion but a lamb. Additionally, the lamb isn't an adult, and the lamb appears to have been slain. This description of the slain Lamb upends Jewish messianic expectations, found in the apocalypses outside the New Testament. For example, 4 Ezra 11–12 presents the messiah as a conqueror, symbolized by a lion. The lion defeats God's enemies and establishes God's kingdom in 4 Ezra. The lamb in Revelation also conquers, but he conquers by dying.

The transformation of the lion into a slain lamb gave Asian Christians a way to understand and withstand their suffering—by following Christ's example. Revelation 1:2; 6:9; 12:11; and 20:4 should be read with this understanding, because victims are transformed into victors (for example, Rev 1:5-6; 5:9-10; 12:11; 19:13; 20:4).

Christ's primary function is to lead the Christian community on a spiritual exodus to the New Jerusalem (for example, Rev 2–3; 7:9-17; 14:1-5; 21:9–22:5). Christ provides benefits for the Christian community. Christ's death brings salvation to the faithful and gathers persons from every ethnic group (compare Eph 2:11-22). While the gathered community is often depicted as a holy army (Rev 14:1-5; 19:14), there is no narrative of a battle. This military imagery symbolizes the difficulty of maintaining Christian practices in an environment hostile to Christian commitments (compare Eph 6:10-20; Matt 10:16-23; Heb 4:12). The true peace of God will remain in the New Jerusalem, devoid of death, sorrow, disease, and pain. It will be perfect forever.

Day 1: Revelation 1–3
John is called.

Revelation 1–3 opens the apocalypse in a unique manner. The presentation of the prophet's visionary call is typical, but the instruction to write to specific contemporary churches (actually delivered by angels to those churches) is unique. These seven messages convey to those particular seven churches what each must do in order to reach the final destination, the New Jerusalem.

The vision described in Revelation 1:12-20 relates directly to the churches. The vision isn't an abstract, otherworldly idea that has little relevance to everyday life. The vision has no meaning apart from the life of the gathered Christian community, then and now. The letters are written to churches, not individuals. To persevere through tough social and political chaos, we do it together, gathered as the church.

As you read each of the seven letters, you will notice a pattern:

1. Jesus affirms praiseworthy strengths of the congregation;
2. Jesus points to areas of weakness in the church;
3. Jesus tells them how to get back on track;
4. and Jesus, like the biblical prophets, describes the negative consequences if they fail and the rewards if they succeed.

Fill out the chart, showing this pattern for each of the seven churches. Ephesus is filled in as an example.

	Praise	Weakness	Remedy	Reward
Ephesus	endurance	lost first love	change heart and life	paradise
Smyrna				
Pergamum				
Thyatira				
Sardis				
Philadelphia				
Laodicea				
My church				

Can you fill in the chart for your own church? Which church of Revelation, if any, is most like your own?

Day 2: Revelation 4:1–8:1
Opening the scroll

Revelation 4 contains a vision of God Almighty being worshipped in the heavenly court. The next chapter introduces a scroll (books with pages appeared after the Bible was written) that must be opened in order to put God's plan for the end of human history in motion. Only the slain Lamb is deemed worthy to open the scroll. The worthiness of the Lamb has come from his sacrificial death, not through military or political power. The Lamb's faithfulness provides a model for Christians to follow (compare Rev 20:4).

The opening of the seven seals launches the divine plan. The apocalyptic visions of Revelation 4–20 represent different versions of a single narrative. This is typical of an apocalypse. However, the repetition gives a novice reader the impression that there are multiple revelations. It's all one revelation. You will often hear people refer to "Revelations" as if it were plural, but that's incorrect. For example, the numbered visions of seals, trumpets, and bowls demonstrate how the intensity of the judgment is growing with each judgment. As another example of emphasis, in Revelation 7:17 and 21:4, God wipes the tears from the faces of the saints.

How is the transformation of the Lion into a Lamb a reversal of human expectations? Are there current or recent Christian movements with militaristic emphases that disagree with this example of the Lamb? Are there contemporary instances in our world where lambs have a more powerful effect than lions?

Day 3: Revelation 12–14
Defeating evil

Revelation 12 presents three visions about the struggle between good and evil. The first vision, Revelation 12:1-6, presents a pregnant woman. In this vision she symbolizes the Virgin Mary and the child Jesus. Satan's harassment of the woman and her child parallels the duress that Asian Christians experienced on earth at that time. The visions in Revelation 7–12 and 13–17 express in different ways this same hatred between Satan and the Christian community. Christians are not only assured of victory, but they are told how to achieve it through a faithful witness, even if it means dying for the faith (Rev 12:11). In fact, Revelation houses the earliest evidence of the use of the word *martyr* in the practical sense of dying for the faith. The Greek word *martyr* means "a witness" or "one who testifies."

While the two beasts of Revelation 13 represent Roman control on land and sea, Revelation 14 presents the Lamb and his heavenly military forces as celibate soldiers purified for battle (compare purity before battle in 1 Sam 21:4-5). However, in chapters 12 and 14, the saints don't engage in a military battle to defeat Satan. Rather, they conquer by means of their witness and their purity (see Rev 12:11; 14:5, 12-13).

You may have heard references to "the one hundred forty-four thousand." This text (Rev 14:3) understandably raises questions for readers. No women are included in the 144,000. In fact, women appear only as agents of defilement in chapter 14, and women are not portrayed in positive terms throughout the whole book of Revelation (compare Rev 17).

Though Revelation contains violent images, and certain interpreters have popularized military implications for the scroll, the message never calls Christians to violence. The slain Lamb calls Christians to nonviolent resistance against an oppressive society or ruler. Revelation teaches us that we are called to faithfully testify and persevere despite the costs. We may not always have the power to change our circumstances or the ability to prevent violence toward us and others, but even then we can choose to act faithfully.

How does Jesus defeat evil today? What particular form of evil concerns you? How do you partner with God in relieving pain and suffering?

Day 4: Revelation 15–17
Seven plagues

While Revelation 15 announces the final numbered series, the series itself begins in chapter 16. This series depicts total destruction of the haughty, power-drunk Roman Empire (symbolized as Babylon, the empire that was the oppressor of the Israelites in the sixth century BCE). Revelation 17 uses the imagery of a prostitute (compare Hos 1–3) as code language for those who know the traditions about the coming end of an oppressive empire.

The woman in Revelation 17 represents the city of Rome as a diabolical power. Rome was and is still known as "the city of seven hills" (see Rev 17:9). Here the heads, mountains, and horns represent Roman rulers. In Episode 23, we noted that a similar imagination is tapped in Daniel 7–11 to describe the empires that oppressed and devastated Israel with exile in the sixth through second centuries BCE. In Revelation, those who cooperate with the empire politically and economically are depicted as irredeemable and are described by means of disturbing violent and sexual metaphors. The author has no sympathy for those who benefit from their relationship with Rome.

The book of Revelation reflects the practice of civil disobedience by resisting the government and the surrounding culture, by naming its injustices and refusing to cooperate and perpetuate the injustice. Revelation assured late first-century Christians that suffering wasn't a result of their unfaithfulness, but rather of their witness and faithfulness. Firm, faithful endurance through suffering results from following the example of Jesus, and that eventually leads to the community's ultimate victory. The crucifixion and the resurrection of Jesus redefined victory for the Christian community and showed God's methods to be opposed to those of Caesar and his empire.

Compare the instruction given in Revelation regarding the relationship between the church and government with the advice given by Paul in Romans 13 or 1 Peter. How does your church bear witness, remain faithful, and help Christ to defeat evil?

Day 5: Revelation 19–22
Final destination

Evil is defeated three times in Revelation 19–20. In the first instance, Christ vanquishes the beast and imprisons him in "the fiery lake that burns with sulfur" (Rev 19:20). In the second, an angel binds Satan for a thousand years (Rev 20:1-4). Finally, Christ defeats Satan and throws him "into the lake of fire and sulfur . . . forever and always" (Rev 20:10).

Now that evil has been defeated permanently, it is time for the New Jerusalem, the final destination of the faithful, to descend to earth. Death, mourning, pain, or anything that prevents abundant life has no place there (Rev 21:4). Moreover, the faithful will be in direct communication with God. An intermediary is no longer necessary. Finally, God will personally console God's people: God "will wipe away every tear from their eyes" (Rev 21:4).

What aspect of your life would you hope to see restored in the New Jerusalem?

Look! I'm making all things new. (Rev 21:5)

Day 6: Revelation 7:9-17
Covenant Meditation: Making us new

As we conclude the Covenant episodes, the theme "New Creation" guides us back to the spiritual reading practice of engaging our imaginations. Revelation presents to us a vision of God's renewed creation. It transforms our hearts and lives, and by God's grace we are equipped through faithful witness in Jesus Christ to help fulfill God's covenantal promises.

But this future, this new creation, is not yet complete. We can't see or experience all that God intends for us and future generations. God continues to make "all things new" in our midst (Rev 21:5). Christ "was and is and is coming" (Rev 4:8*b*). We are still growing and changing in faith, witness, and trust as Christians of the current age who are committed to help the world be transformed by God's love. By using our God-given gift of imagination, we can draw more deeply from the word, testifying to the future that God intends and in which we are called to participate.

For today's reading practice, first move to a place that is quiet, with as few distractions as possible. Before reading, take a moment to prayerfully prepare so that you can approach the scripture as though you have never read it before. Now turn to Revelation 7:9-17.

Read these verses slowly, aloud or silently. Try to put yourself in the scene as the elder who asks the question in Revelation 7:13. Imagine what you see when the great crowd first appears. What do the people look like? What do the languages sound like? What is your first reaction to the crowd that is gathering in front of you? Why do you ask John this particular question? How do you feel when John's response to you is that "you know" (Rev 7:14) who the people are?

Imagine how you feel as you speak about the hardship these people have experienced. What hardships have you witnessed that come to mind as you read this text? Where have you witnessed the need of God's people for shelter and protection that is promised here? Who needs the "springs of life-giving water" (Rev 7:17) today, and what is this water? Whose tears do you pray that God will wipe away? How do you imagine God wiping away these tears? As you close this reading time, offer a prayer of gratitude for God's covenant promise in which you have a part.

Group Meeting Experience

Our covenant

Your group will share a meal and something each person has learned that will help you live together as Covenant people. What did *covenant* mean to you when you started? What does it mean now?

Your leader will also facilitate a time of commitment and prayer. Come prepared to share a story or memory of your time together and what steps you can take to help each other continue on the path of faithful life in Jesus. More concretely, think of the gifts and graces you see in the people in your group. How have they blessed your life? How have they challenged you? What will you do to stay connected to them?

SIGNS OF FAITHFUL LOVE

We put our hope and trust in Christ's ultimate victory over evil. We go into our communities to alleviate suffering and do all the good that we can.

Well done!

You have completed the third and final participant guide, *Trusting the Covenant*. You studied daily from scripture about the importance of trusting God even when the world comes apart. And in your Covenant group, you discovered the gifts and graces of friends for life. You will not be the same!

Your daily habit for reading scripture will continue to shape your life in powerful ways. The relationships you have formed will last into eternity. And you are empowered to share some of what you have learned through service to your church, community, and world.

The Bible is a conversation partner for life. While you can never plumb all of its depths, you have found a way to make sense of the big ideas that create a pattern for a living response to God's faithful love. God's call and promise—that you belong to a place and people who share your mission to help the hurting and the lost—has never been more clear in your life. Now is the time to discover how God's unique design of your gifts and passions will help you live as a committed disciple of Jesus Christ.

You will want to visit CovenantBibleStudy.com and explore some of the tools for plotting your part in God's ongoing salvation story. God's plan for restoring the world has you cast in a leading role!

www.ingramcontent.com/pod-product-compliance
Lightning Source LLC
Chambersburg PA
CBHW081921180426
43200CB00032B/2905